HELLO, FROM SOMEWHERE:

STORIES OF THE ROADS I TRAVELED

(A Memoir)

METTY PELLICER

DEDICATION

TO ALL AFFLICTED WITH WANDERLUST

ACKNOWLEDGMENT

Books in my childhood that inspired curiosity, thirst for adventure and wanderlust to see other lands and people
Scheherazade and 1001 Nights, Nancy Drew and Hardy Boys Series, A Tree Grows in Brooklyn
My friends who encouraged me to write about my travels and demanded that I compile them into this book.
My Starbuck Writing Group and Marley's Critique Group for their support and helpful feedback

TABLE OF CONTENTS

INTRODUCTION

During WWII, the Philippines was a US territory. After the bombing of Pearl Harbor and of Clark Field in the Philippines, the Japanese made a land invasion in Lingayen Gulf and occupied the Philippines in 1942-1945. My father was working in the Mountain Province, in Kalinga, in the Cordilleras in northern Luzon and I was growing in my mother's womb. I'd heard stories of how Mama and Papa trekked from the mountains to Pasacao, in the Bicol peninsula in southern Luzon, to reunite with family during those uncertain times. On the long foot journey they stopped at farms and small villages and obtained food and shelter purely out of kindness of strangers, all the while evading the Japanese. In Pasacao, my grandparents and uncles and some friends hid in the deep jungle of Suminabang, to wait out the war. There they established a self-contained community where they hunted, farmed and fished and life continued. I was born there, in Suminabang. After the war, Papa went to work in Mindanao, the southernmost big island. He was a surveyor. He opened the forests with roads for a foreign owned lumber company which harvested its timber. He left us with my grandparents while he prepared a place for us. My first memory of travel was the voyage we took when Papa summoned us to join him.

I was six years old. We sailed on a steamship from Manila in Luzon to Misamis Occidental in Mindanao. My sister Nancy was four and Hazel was barely two. Papa was away already for a year, so Mama had her hands full. The trip took several days and nights. We were on the deck of the ship and slept on canvas cots in a common area. One day the sea was wild, with howling winds and giant waves, and torrential rain which hammered the ship in all direction. Everybody was throwing up. I was seaworthy, trained well by *Itay*, my grandfather, who was a fisherman, and who took me with him to visit his deep sea fish corrals, *palaisdaan*. He said, "Always keep your eyes on the horizon, and you won't get sick."

I couldn't wait to arrive at our destination. I was excited and curious and I fitted in quickly. In two months I was fluent with the Cebuano dialect and interpreting for Mama, playing with the local kids, and hitchhiking lumber trucks to and from school, which was several kilometers away. So my first memory of travel was of a grand adventure, and of having new friends.

And so I was bursting with excitement again when my father got a new job and we moved back to Luzon island, this time to Larap, in Camarines Norte, where my father worked as an engineer in the Philippine Iron Mines, an American owned company which exported iron ore to Japan. When my father traveled to Japan and came back bearing gifts of pearls, Imari tea set, silks, lacquerware, and Diorissimo, it planted the seed of desire in me to go and see the places where these fabulous things came from. I read books and imagined seeing myself in these lands.

While growing up in the coastal village of Pasacao, nobody traveled. But Mama opened up our world by packing us on a train to Manila to see the Circus and the blockbuster Hollywood movie, The Ten Commandments. Emigration made the dream of seeing the world a reality. As soon as I obtained US citizenship I started traveling, even before I could afford it. I was like Susan Sontag who said, "I haven't been everywhere, but I'm working on it." And it felt like Dr. Seuss was addressing me, "Oh, the places you'll go!"

"There is fun to be done!" -Dr. Seuss

CHAPTER 1: A Party to Remember

To celebrate my retirement from thirty-six years of medical practice, I booked my friend Delia's five-bedroom villa in Monte Pego, in Costa Blanca, on the Spanish Mediterranean Coast. Delia and I went back all the way from Baltimore, where I did my General Psychiatry Residency and Child Psychiatry Fellowship at Sheppard-Pratt Hospital in 1968-1972. After I moved to Atlanta in 1980, she had often invited me but our busy schedules never meshed. She and her villa immediately came to mind when I began to think about how to mark this chapter of my life.

I wanted a celebration to remember. I had a large private practice until managed care health insurance became the norm. It imposed mandates on my clinical practice which forced me to choose between services to patients and reimbursement. Jay-Jay and Doobie have graduated from college, and Johnny and I were empty nesters. I did not need a big practice and could downsize to a salaried hospital staff position until my full retirement age in ten years. I wouldn't need to deal with insurance companies and reimbursements, and I could just concentrate on treating patients as I saw fit. An ideal position opened up at Georgia Regional Hospital as the Director of the new Child Psychiatry Inpatient Unit. This went well. I was happy in my position until the last two years. Because I protested loudly the staffing cut backs that impacted patient care adversely, I earned a place as thorn on the side of administration. Work politics became unbearable. I couldn't give in to the reckless impulse to quit and throw away retirement benefits from the State which I would qualify to receive in twelve months. I felt trapped and suffocated, demeaned, and powerless. I had to harness support and strength from my friends and family. And so when my tenth employment anniversary arrived on August 31, 2008 I couldn't wait to check out. I discouraged any farewell party plans. I was not cut out to be politically correct. When my colleagues looked at me with pitying eyes and made remarks as if I was going to be lost in long days of emptiness and boredom, I sent them a cheery card bidding adieu to the tune of Evita's aria, "Don't cry for me GRH-Atlanta, the truth is I couldn't wait to leave you!"

After I signed off at Personnel, cleaned out my desk, and turned in my badge and keys, I rolled the top down of my Beetle convertible and drove off into the brilliant sun, my hair blowing in the wind, and my joy soaring with Beethoven's Violin Concerto in D major playing on NPR. Free at last!

I had a grand retirement party planned for months. I had this idea that I should be a nomad for a while, living for months at a time in a single country and really getting to know the place and the people and experiencing how they live. It turned out that a lot of people were already doing this as a lifestyle. I started corresponding by email with one of them, Rita Golden Gelman. I wanted to meet her while she was in Atlanta but our schedules didn't merge. I could be a dilettante nomad, that was it! So I planned right away to be abroad in September and October with the first month to be my grand retirement party in Costa Blanca. I rented Delia's five-bedroom villa and I invited all my friends to join me. Twenty-three signed up.

It turned out that Costa Blanca was populated mostly by English expatriates who had transformed the coast into a homogeneous strip of high rise condominiums. Their cookie cutter luxury villas each with backyard swimming pools covered the hills of Monte Pego. There was no opportunity to get acquainted with the local culture as the neighbors were English and friends streamed in throughout the four weeks. The indigenous population in the interior villages became the tourist attraction together with the Roman and Moorish ruins dotting the coast. So OK, this was a party. My nomadic experiment would have to be launched yet.

I had all the arrivals on a calendar grid, and I had a map laid out on the dining table to mark the places we'd visit with colored pins. But Kathy and Susan arrived on the day before I thought they would. They didn't have the villa address and had no clue how to get there. They tried to call me, but got my voicemail. Meanwhile their phones were on low battery and so they decided to call Dick, Susan's husband who was in Atlanta, to get in touch with me. Dick had no idea how so he got a hold of Anicia, who was going to join our party in a few days, to follow-up. Meanwhile Susan and Kathy were trying to charge their phones and was looking for a charging station but they couldn't communicate in Spanish. Susan thought she could demonstrate by holding her left index finger and thumb in a circle and moving her right index finger in and out of the hole to suggest an electric socket. She got a smirk and a quizzical look. Between Dick and Anicia calling back and forth I finally got the message, and unable to reach Susan and Kathy by phone, I decided to drive to Valencia even if it was very late. It was close to midnight when I arrived and the airport was closed but I found a security guard who let me in to see if my people would be among the passengers sleeping inside. I examined every snoring body prostrate on benches and on the floor and not finding them I concluded that they were big girls and would know to book a nearby hotel for the night. The landlady, who Anicia finally contacted, came by early in the morning to deliver the message that Kathy and Susan were at Hotel Ibis. Later, this misadventure evolved into highly entertaining cocktail vignettes at dinner parties, told over and over again. We got full mileage out of the tale. To cap the day's excitement, Evelyn, famous for her photographic memory, recognized Susan instantly, a colleague from work twenty-five years ago, an old friend rediscovered. Small world indeed.

The next day Anicia and Diane arrived, but not their luggage, and it wasn't delivered until two days later. We already scheduled a trip to the flea market in Benidorn so this would be a good place to pick up some necessary supplies. This is a big one and with lots of English antiques and stuff since the town is mostly populated by them. I got a sterling necklace of a flying unicorn and a 1920 brooch with mink and pearls, very chic. Anicia got a bathing suit, one size smaller for $3. I suggested that she may need to lubricate it with baby powder, teasing that it was mine if it didn't fit her. She was determined and wiggled and held her breath to squeeze into it.

In the afternoon we went to the beach in Denia, the main town nearest Monte Pego, then picked fresh fish from the market to grill at Delia's villa and watch the sunset there. Delia got her two villas precisely for their orientation to the sun, rising in Villa Delchel, where we were staying and to the sunset in Bella Ocaso. The following day Delia took us to Guadalest, to visit the castle and to view the amazing valley and mountains and river encircling the fortress like a moat, its water the color of jade. We had lunch there, and celebrated Susan's birthday. She got an enormous red lollipop to lick for a year until her next birthday. Intoxicated by nature's beauty, we overindulged and so we were lucky to have Diane who is allergic to alcohol, our designated driver. Mary gave me a GPS, my retirement gift. We named her Petra and she took us around the scenic route going back to the villa. She was really getting to know us and finally became a reliable friend and guided us safely. When we first activated her for duty, on the twisting roads of Monte Pego at night, she directed us to plunge into the ravine. Driving from Seville to Alhambra in Granada, she steered us towards Madrid. We didn't know that there are many Alhambras in Spain. Realizing this after two hours, we corrected her, but then she had us drive up the narrow cobblestone alleys of Albayzin, the medieval village along the route to Alhambra, only to be met with frantic waving of the hands and wide-eyed warnings to stop and turn around by the pedestrians. We learned that vehicles are strictly forbidden and the Alhambra had to be approached from the highway. After this yet another faux pas, we renamed her Bitch. However on this Guadalest trip, she took us seamlessly up and down two mountains to go home. Climbing to the peak, the nearly full silver moon emerged before us while the setting sun left muted reflections of purple and oranges and reds in the back drop, like a painted landscape. It was so dramatic it moved us to sing songs with moon themes. I started off with made up lyrics, only remembering the melody, but the gang quickly guessed and put words to Harbor Lights. We sang Moon River with complete lyrics, and followed with Fly Me To The Moon, Full Moon and Empty Arms, By the Light of the Silvery Moon, how about that!

Next came Pauline, my niece, with her five girlfriends. They were refused boarding in Barcelona without a printed ticket, the virtual ticket on their smart phone would not do, and the others had their tickets packed in their luggage. It took a while looking for a printer, they missed two trains, and therefore were late arriving in Valencia. By this time I had information on a nearby train station, Xeroca to pick up arrivals, only thirty minutes away, compared to two hours if I pick up in Valencia. It required a transfer to a local train in Valencia. I sent a text message:

You're on the train already from Barcelona, you'd be in the station in Valencia Nord, transfer to the train to GANDIA and get off XEROCA, 45 MIN TRIP, THEN I CAN PICK YOU UP AT XEROCA, train leaves every 30 minutes.

They missed two departures, and arrived in the evening, but they were cool. No worries. The following day they slept in and hung out in the pool. They announced that they'd prepare dinner so we drove to Denia to market and to pick up some wine. The bodegas of Valencia, Alicante and Murcia, are producing wines that's starting to rival the great producing regions of La Rioja. Its tintos, tempranillos, grenaches and chardonnays were cheap and plentiful, and as good as they come. We had a wonderful meal, they giggled and shrieked all night, and next day, the trash was full of empty wine bottles. Ahh, to be young. Then they were off on their own to overnight in Alicante and I was left alone for the first time since I arrived.

I decided to check out the fiesta in Vall DÉbo. Arriving at midday, there was nothing going on but a few people congregating at a bar-restaurant in the tiny main square. I thought maybe I had the wrong date or the fiesta was not starting until the evening. Teens were transporting chairs probably for the supposed free supper. Anyway it was a lovely little village, of seven hundred inhabitants according to the brochure, no Englishman there, and no one spoke English. I walked into the bar-restaurant and watched what people were eating, talked with the owner and a few patrons. They were very friendly but my poquito castilian espanol and their valencian dialect made conversation laborious. However the grilled lamb chops and the olleta alicantina, a vegetarian stew of chickpeas, lentils, chard, potato, beets, turnip, green beans, tomato, typical in the mountain areas, were pure gastronomic delight. I decided to drive to the next village to check out the stalactites and stalagmites of Cova del Rull. I explored the little mountain villages along the way. It was a Sunday, the village people were milling around the church square. It framed an idyllic scene with the rose-colored terra cotta cottages, on a backdrop of lush green pastures under a tranquil blue sky. The drive back was on knuckle-whitening serpentine roads, more steep and formidable than the return trip from Guadalest, with plunging ravines, literally breathtaking. Arriving in Monte Pego I decided to tour the other villas, weaved in and out of narrow side streets to check them out but turned into the wrong street to my villa. I chose to back up, instead of making a U-turn. I failed reverse driving maneuvers in my licensing test and I've gotten used to having rear view lookouts when everybody was around, so predictably, I hit the stone wall. My rental Renault Picasso's tail was badly disfigured and I scraped the rear tire so deeply it tore. I could not drive on those mountains with the inflatable spare tire. The car was un-drivable and it took until four PM next day to get a replacement vehicle. I was marooned in the villa. I filed my nails, floated in the pool, read, and a mistake, watched CNN and got the bad news. The US was leading the world to a financial crisis with the mortgage debt debacle, the bail out of Fannie Mae and Freddie Mac, and the collapse of Lehman Brothers. Wall Street was seizing as the stock market plunged, and property values hit an all time low. I had just retired and had become dependent on my 401K. Aaarghh! I reminded myself, "I'm having a party, I'll think about it when the party's over." As Scarlett would say, "Tomorrow is another day." Thank goodness the girls had surplus wine and leftovers. I had a new silver Picasso delivered the next day.

Marites and company flew into Valencia, and decided they will rent their own car. In addition, the girls, who were visiting Valencia asked to ride back with them. I was on the golf course in Xavea, La Sella, designed by Jose Maria Olazabal, where I shot a 47 on the front and collapsed at the back. I texted directions:

*Driving from Valencia, in the direction of Alicante, you exit on #63 Oliva-Pego exit, then go through the town of Oliva, look for the small sign to Pego on right , then after you get out of the town, **look for the very, very small sign to Pego on your left.** Once you're on this road, follow it until Bella Vista, go up the mountain and on top turn left where there is a big sign board of the development, follow to the end of the road where the Bella Vista restaurant is, turn right there and follow the road as it curves right and just go straight until it ends to Villa Delchel. Text me of exact arrival.*

Myrna was driving and missed the very, very small sign to Pego just outside the town of Oliva. Before leaving Valencia she was already rattled by the round-abouts and kept on exiting the wrong road. This stretch of road was narrow and isolated, and very dark at night, but as there were eight people in the car, they were nonplussed. Myrna couldn't make a U-turn on the narrow road so she decided to back up but found out she could not put the gears on reverse. Illuminated by the headlights, one of the girls read the Spanish manual while another translated, and Myrna tried to execute. Manolo in the meantime, sensing that his bladder was ready to burst,: decided to relieve himself on the roadside just as one of the girls happened to turn her head and confronted the spectacle. Myrna could not find the reverse button as the manual described but by helplessly fumbling with the gears, she felt a small indentation on the knob and when she pushed her finger into it, the car automatically went on reverse!

Niti and Susan N. flew into Alicante, and they too rented a car. They had a GPS but it did not have the European application. To everyone's incredulity, they found their way to the villa, the old-fashioned way, with a map! Evelyn and Chai got lost in Alicante on their way to Madrid. They couldn't find the train station and were driving around in circles for an hour, asked several people but they kept on getting lost. Time was running out for boarding. Waiting at a red light, they asked a well-dressed Spaniard in a Mercedes convertible. Like a knight in shining armor, he came to their rescue. He guided them into the station with plenty of time left before departure. Meanwhile, in Madrid, Myrna got robbed of her wallet with thousands in cash, her credit cards and passport. In Barcelona, a nimble thief snatched the purse of one of the girls while strolling in the Barri Gotic, and swiftly disappeared into the crowd.

"Waiting for a Train to Get On" -Dr. Seuss

CHAPTER 2: On The Thrill Track

It was a thrill when I first got on a train. I was barely six years old. I'd see the big creature rounding the bend like a centipede, its head belching smoke and its tail coiling behind it. It will approach with a steady beat, chug! chug!, and as it nears the station its whistle will blow, hoot! hoot!, then it will unleash the brassy urgent warning of its bell, clang! clang!, before it exhales its final breath, swoooosh! shhh! and come to rest to take in passengers into its belly. One day Mama announced we're going to Manila to see the circus. Wonders of wonders! That meant we were going on a train. Manila is another world. We almost peed in our pants in excitement.

The trip took the entire day or overnight. Mama was careful with money, she bought third class coach tickets. We sat among sacks of rice and bananas, and crates of chickens, and during train stops, we hailed food vendors. We extended half of our bodies out of the window and bought treats like steamed cakes *puto, suman, and maruya,* deep fried bananas. I've loved trains since, they promised something wonderful or the unexpected at the end of the line.

On my first trip to France, I took the TGV from Paris to Lyon to dine at the ultra uppity eatery presided by Paul Bocuse, Auberge du Pont de Collonges. The meal and wine pairings cost me an arm and a leg and a bruised pride. The establishment is very elegant and the cuisine Michelin-starred. An amuse-bouche served with a flourish announced the grand gastronomic experience to follow. Even the citrusy sorbet palate cleanser seemed special. Then the impressive cheese cart was rolled in followed by chocolates. At this point I asked for coffee which our waiter greeted with a raised eyebrow and hesitation conveying clearly that I was out of order. When I firmly held to my request with a smile, he grandly complied with a huff. I was supposed to have my coffee after dessert, which followed the chocolate. I'm always learning new things when traveling.

I did not have reserved seats when I hopped on the train to Avignon from Paris, and found out that the train was full. There were mostly young people on board, many just sat on the floor for the three-hour trip, and were eager to practice their English. The time went by in a click as we tackled various topics while scenes of the bucolic countryside rolled as the train sped by. A surprise awaited me in Avignon. This was before smartphones and iPads became a traveler's knowledgeable companion.

There was a festival. The street was crowded with tourists and costumed performers, many in various stages of undress. There were mohawk hairdos in purple and yellow and fuchsia , and ballerina tutus, medieval costumes, multicolored clowns prat-falling for laughs, poetry in a corner, strolling musicians, and ticket vendors for the theatrical productions on stage all over town. Painters were covering sidewalks with graffiti art and everyone mooching and cheery and friendly. The cafes and restaurants were full and there was no place to sleep for the night. I found a Bed and Breakfast in the outskirts which was quite charming and the proprietors were very helpful in spite of our mutual language handicap and the French reputation for unfriendliness. Visiting the medieval gothic Palais des Papes, the object of my trip was anticlimactic.

Some years later, I was in Costa Blanca and I took the Euromed first class from Alicante to Barcelona. It was a high speed train, pristine and sleek, with beautiful interior, in-seat dining, and hostess service. I short cut through France to Italy on a ferry to continue my journey by train. From Barcelona, the ferry crossed the Mediterranean to Genoa, a sixteen-hour trip which took twenty hours due to headwinds. The ferry arrived at dusk with the last glimmer of light disappearing behind the Apennine mountains and reflecting muted oranges and reds in the darkening sky. The city wrapped in lights ascending to the hills was shimmering like jewels, its image mirrored on the water. Genoa is Christopher Columbus' birthplace, an intimate link between the Old and the New World.

I was admiring the palaces along Via Garibaldi on my way to Via della Maddalena to visit its namesake church when a well-dressed gentleman with a British accent matched his steps with me and started a conversation. He seemed to be a salaried man on a business trip, but his manner was unusually familiar for a casual chitchat between tourists. When I came to my street and was about to turn he followed suit and seemed to indicate he'd be with me. I firmly said goodbye which he obeyed without protest. Via della Maddalena traversed very narrow cobblestone alleys with decaying buildings, and some with collapsed roofs revealing dumped thrash and foraging alley cats. Along this ancient road were women in very short and tight shape-defining clothes, heavily made up and assuming sexually suggestive poses outside decrepit buildings. I saw a few go indoors accompanied by a man. The young women were mostly Africans and Southeast Asians, and it dawned on me that I must have been mistaken for one of them. How appropriate that they are practicing their profession on this street, and how marvelous that I can turn a trick at my age without even trying.

In Italy the Frecciarossa trains are their French TGV counterparts, sleek with speeds up to 210 miles per hour, and comfortable even with second class seats. While many find France intriguing and romantic, I rather like Italy's hot and brash temperament. Rome's more familiar history, as connected with the bible and the popular Verdi and Puccini operas adds further weight in my esteem.

From Genoa it's a one and a half hour trip on a Frecciabianca train to Milan. I wanted to see Leonardo da Vinci's Last Supper but I didn't know that admission was limited and required advanced reservation which can have a six-month wait. So I went on to Verona to visit Juliet's tomb, then from Milan took the Frecciarossa high speed train to Naples, my launching point for Pompeii, Ischia, and Sorrento.

First I had to learn to say and use PREGO. I heard it a lot. Arriving at a restaurant, the maitre invited me to a table and said Prego, he smiled and said Prego while handing me a menu, after I ordered he said once more, Prego. A gentleman opened the door for me, he said Prego as he let me pass, and I heard it when the concierge answered the phone, Prego. It does not mean one thing and is used for a lot of things, anyway, I think I got the drift, so when I sent out emails I opened with Prego Y'all!

I got to Napoli and proceeded to Vesuvius. First I took the Metro from my hotel to Piazza Garibaldi then connected with the suburban train, Circumvesuviana Railway, and got off at Ercolano-Scavi station, where a shuttle bus took me to Vesuvius. That was the easy part. I wasn't prepared to hike up the volcano crater for forty minutes. I was so out of shape without my regular workout this past six weeks, eating pasta and all, so I was huffing and puffing. It was profound to circle the outer rim and view the caldron crater and contemplate that the violent cataclysm of its eruption buried the whole city of Pompeii and Herculaneum in 79 AD. So I got on the train again to see Pompeii, the ash covered city preserved in its time by the eruption, and informs us in modern times how life was lived long ago. I didn't realize this excavation is so immense and mind-boggling. It is an entire city, so awesome. I had a hard time getting out of there. I got lost in the maze of streets and alleys. Of note, the whorehouse, with frescoes of all the different ways you can copulate. Too bad I didn't know how to set my camera without flash, so I wasn't able to take pictures. Then there was this painting of Priapus, the god of fertility, he's the one we derived the word priapism from. He's there with his grotesquely oversized penis laid out on a plate. These early Romans really knew how to live and that we're not so different in our aspirations in our lifestyle today. I admired how their houses were laid out, with opulent parlors and verandahs and courtyards and gardens. And the baths, and the rituals associated with it, cold dips, tepid dips and hot dips, none of these quick utilitarian showers we modern agers take without ceremonies, and the tactile luxury that goes with unguents, and liniments and fragrances slathered and massaged on the skin. Bathing can take up half a day. What a life! Then since the end of the line is to Sorrento, I decided to take the train to the end. Sorrento is charming and of course has an emotional tug with the familiar songs *Come Back to Sorrento, and O Sole Mio*, so it had me before I could even say, "Prego". The train trip back to the hotel was over one hour, what with changes and all, so I had a late dinner at the hotel before they closed the kitchen at 10:30 pm. I stayed up late for the US Vice Presidential debates, which were at 2 am here. I had never heard of this woman Sarah Palin until now and it's sad that we are reduced to picking for national leadership a small fish from a small pond. Ischia, with its thermal springs and spas, was just the appropriate destination after this arduous day and I have to be up early the following day.

There's so many hustlers in Naples, and you have to be alert, and the city is littered in many places, and graffiti is everywhere, but it is vibrant and bustling and bold and macho, it is so alive, it's like New York. It is also culturally diverse with Senegalese, Ukrainians and Polish taking up the unskilled workforce. It feels familiar like Manila, with macho men, and over-the-top glitz, and bambinas sexed to the hilt. TV news anchors of middle aged men with paunchy middles have sidekicks of Bimbo types with low necklines and silicon boobs and tight or short short skirts and six-inch platform heels, painted with dark eyeliners and red lips. I missed seeing Penelope Cruz on billboards as I saw her in Spain, elegant, polished and fresh. Billboards here feature lingerie ads with pouty models. In Ischia the social events were fashion shows, and yeah, lingerie shows. Naples is in the process of cleaning itself up. There's public works all over the place and buildings in scaffolds undergoing reinvigorating renovations. I feel a connection with this region with Sorrento and Capri which I've read so much about while in the Philippines. A city with the sea at its doorstep will always have captivating charm for me.

Ischia is about an hour by ferry from Naples, in sight of Vesuvius across the bay. It is called the green island because in contrast to rocky Capri, Ischia is covered with vegetation. There are thermal locations all over the island. The ground water is heated, there are thermal sands, and even the seawater in some areas is heated by volcanic action. Almost all the hotels (and there are many) have pools that are heated by geo-thermal heat. Poseidon Gardens and Negombo are places you can go to spend the day in the thermal pools and also in the sea, because both have lovely beaches in addition to the pools. Though Capri is more famous, Ischia gained some popularity with the release of Matt Damon's *The Talented Mr. Ripley*. The naturally calibrated thermal pools and jacuzzis are heavenly, and after my bio-energy massage and pampering at the Poseidon Beach and Spa, all my aches from lugging my suitcase in train stations and ferries have disappeared.

I took a public bus around the island, covering the coast and the interior to the highest point. It took about three hours and two Eu1.20 tickets good for ninety minutes ride each. It was a great tour and the local passengers were knowledgeable guides. The roads here are so tight, the bus had to stop every time there was an approaching car. A dog jumped off from an oncoming tri-scooter and our bus hit the poor thing and looked like its leg was broken and its hip dislocated. We were all upset. Tourists are mainly Germans here, they even have a German TV channel. The average mature woman is heavily made-up, favors shiny and loud wardrobe, with emphasis on tight and cleavage exposure.

Men on the beach have beer bellies and wiggly buns and fronts encased in skimpy, organ shape-defining jersey swim trunks. Hardly an inspiring vision. My friends have fantasized a romantic adventure for me and how could I possibly have prospects with this sample?

My villa is on top of the hill, with spectacular views and there is a little town, ten-minute walk away with a restaurant and mercado. Next door is an internet lounge where all the village teens congregate to play video games. I got to be friends with the restaurant owners, a young couple with elementary aged children. Italian seems more manageable plus body language in conversation than French.

Much later in my travels, in Japan, language was no barrier in appreciating the clock efficiency of its Shinkansen. Accurate to the second, the sleek, bullet-like train approached with the speed of sound and could be seen before it was heard. Swoosh and there it goes. I only saw its end receding in a blur before I realized it had passed. I took the Shinkansen from Osaka to Kyoto. I started in a metropolis of skyscrapers and man-made island and arrived in a magical place from long ago, filled with thousands of Shinto and Buddhist shrines, magnificent gardens, natives strolling in traditional kimonos, and ancient streets lined with wooden houses continuously occupied from centuries ago. The geisha district of Gion recalled for me the novel, Memoirs of a Geisha, a fascinating tale, and dramatized my exploration. I can't wait for another train to get on!

"A Journey Is Best Measured In Friends, Rather Than Miles." -Tim Cahill

CHAPTER 3: The Friends I Made

I lost my best travel buddy when Johnny died. He was the ideal companion. He let me choose our destination, and make the basic arrangements. He did not quibble about the must sees I wanted, and once we reached our location he could come up with exciting ways to experience the place, because he had skills I did not possess and was endowed with a livelier imagination for adventure. On a Greek Islands Cruise, we wanted to get away from the bustle of the tourist areas in Rhodes. We rented a motorcycle and explored nearby beaches and rocky bays, and chose a small hidden sandy cove to relish a picnic lunch, watch the waves lap the shore and make love. On a trip to the south of France we rented a stick-shift open roadster, and with care-free invincibility burned the tires on the Corniche to Monaco, and soaked in the allure of its myth. In Scotland, on a golfing trip to the venerable St Andrew's Golf Course, our B&B at Elie on the Firth of Forth, was next to a pub stocked with one-hundred different distillations of single malt whiskey. We sampled each bottle until we'd tasted each and every kind.

I've traveled solo since Johnny passed. My friends got all very excited about the prospect for romantic adventures on these trips, but so far I've only disappointed them. I harbored no such fantasies. Unlike women of any age, men near my age did not travel solo. They were dead or too macho to feel unmoored in a foreign land.

But meeting all sorts of different people is a byproduct of travel and solo travel proved to be the perfect formula for making friends in the most unexpected ways.

I volunteered as an English speaker in an immersion language program, Pueblo Ingles, in La Alberca, Spain. In exchange for my skill, I was provided free lodging and meals for the week-long course. All I was required to do was to converse in English with the Spaniards who were managers or executives in multinational companies, who needed the language expertise in their work. The English speakers were from Canada, England, South Africa, Israel, and the US. I was one of three speaking English as a second language, the other two were originally from Sri Langka and Israel. The others from the US were from Birmingham and Peachtree City, in Atlanta.

La Alberca, in the province of Salamanca, is a medieval village of 1000 people that is listed in the National Historic Registry. Its well-preserved town square with its gothic church is still the hub of activity. Pigs roam freely in the square. They are a special breed of pigs fed exclusively with black acorns, raised here to produce the most expensive ham in the world, Jamon Iberico, Pata Negra. Surrounding the village are acorn, and chestnut and birch forests and granite mountains. Then there are the farms and pig and bull paddocks, where the toros used in bullfighting are bred. It is a Spain seldom experienced by tourists.

Sequestered in this remote location and engaged in an intense activity, I soon became part of a close-knit group. I exchanged visits with new friends made from Birmingham, AL and Peachtree City. When I made a trip to Madrid and Barcelona years later, I had a reunion with the Spanish friends I made. In the interim I visited the friend from Israel, in Tel Aviv, which happened to be during Passover. She brought me to her father's kibbutz in Kissufim, located in the Negev desert, one mile from the Gaza Strip. My US friends were afraid for me as the kibbutz was within bombing distance from the Gaza strip, but since my friend's father lived there I figured I would be safe. A bomb shelter is in each home. This again was a unique experience of the place not afforded the ordinary tourist. It was the first time I attended a Seder. It is a ritual feast with symbolic food and ceremony prescribed from the holy book Haggadah, commemorating the Exodus, the liberation of the Israelites from slavery in ancient Egypt. It is celebrated in the evening of the fifteenth day of the Nisan calendar, roughly corresponding to late March or April of the Gregorian calendar. It is observed by Jews the world over. With multigenerational representation the youngest child would ask the ritual "Four Questions", the first one being, "Why is this night different from all other nights?" The answers to these questions affirm Jewish identity and faith for subsequent generations. Among the symbolic foods on my Passover Seder plate were, bitter herbs, lamb, hard-boiled egg, sweet fruit paste, salt, a separate stack of matzo bread, all flushed down with four cups of wine. I was enthralled and drunk!

After I left the kibbutz, I joined a group tour of Israel and Egypt. A couple from Brisbane became good friends and when I visited Australia, we made plans to get together. I was made to feel like a part of the family. I met their children, all daughters. One was going to Israel to volunteer, another was auditioning for an opera, and the youngest was still in high school. I had meals in their home, tagged along to her choir practice, met her friends and visited with her mother who lived in a plush condominium on the banks of the Brisbane River, in the heart of downtown.

And friendships snowballed from there.

I had a childhood friend in Sydney so I contacted her for lodging recommendations. She referred me to her friend who owned a hotel with her boyfriend in Coogee Beach. The boutique hotel was perfect, right on the beach, near the bus stop to Sydney, and served French pressed coffee and continental breakfast in a beautiful garden room. I was traveling in an open ended manner, without an itinerary and booking hotels along the way as I decided on my next destination. When my hosts, who at this time were already my friends, learned that my next location was the Great Barrier Reef, they prevailed upon me not to book a hotel pending contact with the boyfriend's ex-wife, who lived in Port Douglas, gateway to the Great Barrier Reef. His ex-wife was delighted to host me at her home. Her contemporary house was on a hill with a view of the Coral Sea. She had a glass-enclosed guest pavilion with one wall facing the ocean and the rest surrounded by the jungle. When I stepped into the bathroom I felt like I was in the middle of the rainforest. She had an infinity pool connecting the guest pavilion and her private quarters and the main house. Immersing ourselves nude into the pool and swimming at eye level with the ocean it seemed like we were in the middle of the Coral Sea. There was no one else but us. At night the sounds of the sleeping rainforest, the rush of cascading water on the walls of the pool, the drone of the cicadas and the hum of the breeze on the trees, lulled me to sleep. The laughing kookaburra sounded the wake-up call, and the slithering salamander in the shower stall reminded me where I was.

The snowball continued to roll and gather mass. Another friend of a friend offered to host me in Melbourne. One call and it was all arranged. She was delighted to have me, a complete stranger, on the word of her friend. Her ultra-sophisticated condominium just outside the city center was close to the train stop. She and her boyfriend were hosting a cocktail party during my visit. Harry Connick was all over the news with his unamused reaction as a guest during a special anniversary reunion of a popular TV show in the 90's, "Hey Hey, It's Saturday". It featured a parody of Michael Jackson, Jackson Jive, in blackface. The spirited exchange about being Aussie and how race was experienced in each country was absorbing and highlighted the evening gathering.

I was traveling solo when I arrived in Sydney. At my last stop, Tasmania, I had a travel buddy, my Coogee hotelier. Wanderlust spreads fairy dust.

I wandered into a small French cafe in a quiet residential side street in Munich after I had explored an intimate park with a small church and cemetery across it. I took the last table outdoors on the narrow patio. As I waited for my order to arrive, a woman approached who inquired if she may share the table. Our rapport was spontaneous, and the conversation came easily. As I had just taken up painting and was interested in the German expressionists, she told me about the Buchheim Museum, one hour by train from Munich, north of Bernried in Höhenried Park, directly on the banks of Lake Starnberg. My visit there was indelible, for the exalting experience of viewing a large collection of the Brucke expressionists. Our conversation absorbed us until the cafe closed its kitchen, but not before we made plans to meet again. Her niece, a flutist was having a benefit concert in the city outskirts, in a former palace with formal gardens, maintained as a venue for intimate chamber music. We met in her apartment and her sister, who was the mother of the flutist, picked us up in her car. I then met their 83-year old mother. She gave me a poem she wrote when I left. Written in German, I had a friend translate it into English. It was a lyrical paean to the simple wonders of a dew drop, the fragrance of a meadow, in a journey of a thousand steps. After four years, my friend wrote that her mother died peacefully in her sleep. She shared with me that her mother was delighted and very proud that her poem was translated into another language.

I signed up for a week of intensive painting workshop in L'Isle-Sur-la-Sorgue, a medieval village in Provence, near Avignon and Gordes. I had never held a paintbrush before nor mixed colors, or ever paid attention to light and shadows. The friendships forged while engaged in a deeply affecting experience were transformative, despite the limitation of language. Our teacher was Italian with a studio in Milan. He was also fluent in French and English, but all his students were Italian. In this group was another Fiammetta, with a double "m" and a double "t", whereas my mother, having had no acquaintance with Boccaccio when she named me, spelled it Fiameta. I've never met another girl named Fiameta. We were both thrilled to discover each other and immediately bonded. She was also a psychiatrist, and already an accomplished painter. She loved opera and when I mentioned I was dying to see one at La Scala, we made plans for me to come to Milan during the season and stay with her. So in no time at all I was in Milan. The week I spent with her family was unforgettable. Furthermore, our painting maestro was informed of my visit, and he invited me to join a class in his studio and to meet his students. He then took me home to his family for dinner. His wife prepared a delicious pasta meal while I played with his two effervescent young daughters. People are amazing with their hospitality and generosity.

As I have no patience for prolonged classroom studies, I signed up in a Spanish immersion program in Cuzco, Peru. The curriculum consisted of a home stay, volunteer work, individualized Spanish instruction, and cultural sightseeing.

My volunteering was a disaster. Without proficiency in the language, I couldn't work with psychiatric patients. The clinic, run by nuns, served the indigenous population, and held weekly outreach into the mountain villages. The nuns didn't know what to do with me, so they had me tag along wherever they went. I accompanied them to visit the mountain tribes, and along the way they showed me archaeological sites that have not been opened to the public yet, and what an incalculable treat that was. I bonded with one sister who was the herbalist. She gave me a priceless education on the native plants and let me help her compound the medicinal herbs into treatments for all manner of ills. Her clinic was busy as the indigenous population still mistrusts modern medicines. Whenever I return to Cuzco, I have a standing invitation for lodging at the Mother House, the restored cloister in the historic square. As well, I will be welcomed by my home stay host, and before my assignment was up we made plans to travel to Brazil. Lodging with me in the host home were two young women from the Netherlands. They were tall, blonde, blue-eyed and full of exuberance, goodwill, and great expectation. Their friendship was rejuvenating. When I was in Madrid, one of the girls was also visiting with her mother. We got together and made further plans for my visit to Amsterdam.

I met a couple on a tour of Colombia, who were from Atlanta, near Cabbage Town. He tinkered with a vintage Chrysler and his partner planted a large vegetable and flower garden. I went to harvest some for my kitchen, cooked them and invited them over for dinner. When they moved to Oaxaca, Mexico I promised to go and visit. I have visited twice already. The expatriate community there is well established and the lifestyle is unique, straddling two different cultures, and I could experience them through my friends without leaving my world.

On a South Pacific cruise, I thought I'd die of boredom until I found a group of party animals who liked to hang out and dance after all the senior passengers had gone to bed. One of the ladies was great fun and easy to be with. I already visited her in San Diego and enjoyed her home and city. Everywhere I travel, there is a friend to be made, and each trip highlight and most exciting adventure is making a new friend. I will make many more. My journey's measure is not the miles I cover but the friends I make.

"I travel not to go anywhere but to go, I travel for travel's sake. The great affair is to move."
- Robert Louis Stevenson

CHAPTER 4: Antarctica

It's the Last Frontier, the Great White Continent, and I've got to go. As everyone is now going to Alaska, going to Antarctica is the last exotic thing to do. The world is getting smaller and smaller, and soon, space will be the next frontier. But for now, it's got to be Antarctica.

Certainly it is not easy to reach Antarctica. Expedition ships to the continent leave from the world's southernmost ports. To get to Ushuaia from Atlanta, you fly to Miami (1 ½ hours), then to Buenos Aires (8 ½ hours), then to Ushuaia (3 ½ hours). Can you imagine the flying hours and routes of those coming from Australia, Korea and India and Norway? Ushuaia, is in the province of Tierra del Fuego in Argentina. These names, along with the Magellan Strait, and Cape Horn are all familiar to me in the history of Philippine colonization by Spain. Without the discovery of these waterways that connect the Atlantic to the Pacific Oceans, our destiny as a country may have been very different. We are told nobody owns Antarctica, that there's a treaty between the countries to ensure that this so, but Argentinian and Chilean children are shown from the first day of school onwards their country's map with Antarctica as part of it.

We embark on our cruise very early in the morning, which requires overnight lodging. All of the accommodations in Ushuaia are booked by the time I tried to call for a reservation, so I wing it on arrival. At the airport I overhear this young woman ahead of me in the line inquire about a hotel room, turns out she is on the same cruise as I am, so we agree to team up and share a room.

The tourist desk recommends an expensive hotel room but she requests a hostel because she's trying to save money. It is fine with me. I've never stayed in a hostel so I am curious. We get a room with two beds and a private bath. After dinner I have no objections to bar hopping for a while. When I realize she is hunting for prey, I leave her to return to the hostel and tell her I'll leave the door unlocked for her. Shuffling sounds and a strong odor wake me up. I open my eyes in the dim light and see her having sexual intercourse in the next bed. It is a small room and the overpowering odor of un-deodorized armpits and unbathed male body is nauseating. I yell at her and ask the obvious, "What the hell are you doing? How dare you! Both of you leave right now, do it elsewhere!" The two leave quickly and without protest but the reeking smell hung in the air permanently. I see her on the ship later and I do not desire further interaction.

The Southern hemisphere is two hours later than EST, and the seasons are reversed as you know. So it's summertime in Antarctica and it's 29-35 degrees F and it's sizzling!

We are told that we are fortunate to have fantastic weather during our voyage. It takes two days and three nights to get out of the Beagle Channel and get onto the Drake Passage then cross the Antarctic Convergence and then finally be in Antarctic waters. In fantastic weather with hardly any wind our little red ship is rocking and see-sawing in billowing waves as big as our ship itself. Everyone has drug-loaded little band-aids stuck behind their ears or are swallowing Dramamine by the fistful. I pride myself as an old salt, having grown up in the coastal village of Pasacao with a fisherman for a grandfather, so I refused drugs, but I yielded to an afternoon in bed to escape the ignominy of shame should I also retch and swoon. The Drake Passage is open sea and notorious for turbulence. There is no scenery, and there's nothing to focus on except the lapping of waves against the hull of the ship. But behold, an albatross! It came from nowhere, and it followed the ship and carried the wind to take us to Antarctica. Pumped up with tales about the albatross and Samuel Taylor Coleridge's The Ancient Mariner, the tour staff, at the conclusion of our voyage, had no problem raising $2700 from the passengers in an auction to save the albatross. The Scot, a passenger who owned a sailboat, bid $1000 for the ship captain's map of our journey.

Finally, land! Er, Ice! We are in Antarctica.

It is very white. Glaciers and ice mountains and sea ice and floating icebergs as far as the eye can see. But if I look closely on a clear day, when snippets of sun-rays come through the continent's perpetual clouds, I can discern subtleties of color. Blue ice shimmers, cascades, and disappears into turquoise water, and emerald waves lap against white monuments that seem to float out of the sea. The landscape is vast, overwhelming, and for the early heroic explorers, inhospitable and tragic. The pristine ice mountains forbid trespassing, the certain outcome of which is death. But we are adventurers in the tourist age, and we arrive in Antarctica in a sturdy Finnish-built expedition cruise ship, the first of its kind. It is our "little red ship," the Explorer. It's small enough to navigate around the ice and get us close enough to shore to land our jaunty ten-man rubber zodiac boats. Unlike the large cruise ships that now also trawl the area, we can explore the continent on terra firma instead of merely watching the scenery through binoculars. In our zodiacs, we stalk the whales until we can catch the shower spray and stink from their breathing holes.

There are no living things on the surface of Antarctica except for cellular organisms. The life is in the waters around it, in the leopard seals, weddell seals, elephant seals, minke whales, and orcas and seabirds. On the continent we made landings in Paradise Harbor, Neko Harbor, Wilhelmina Bay, Aicho, and the Lemaire Channel. The flora and fauna have more variety in the subantarctic islands, such as the South Shetland Islands, with moss vegetation and seabirds such as kelp gull and skuas. Everywhere are Chinstrap penguins, Gentoo penguins, Adelie penguins, Macaroni Penguins. They are interesting to learn about, and a joy to watch, but after seeing one of them I'd felt I'd seen them all. You can only watch penguins do the same things for so long. Besides, the rookery stank to high heaven with a fishy, decomposing odor not unlike bad *bagoong*, a Philippine fermented fish sauce. You would never guess it from the neat, elegant photos these birds appear in.

I began to watch the clock for the next meal. The gourmet meals on board were prepared by a young German cook who had been to Cebu and other parts of the Philippines to recruit kitchen workers. He liked their work ethics and attitude, and the ship crew consisted of thirty-some Pinoys out of a crew of fifty. There were a few second level officers and ship engineers, but most were service staff and entertainers. I got to know most of the crew, with two from Naga City and several from Bicol, my home province. I spent a night playing mahjong in their staff quarters and got beat, but they refused to accept my money, so I didn't join them when they invited me back for *tong-it*, a card game. But they had *calderetta* one night and that was a welcome culinary break from the gourmet fare in the dining room.

I was the lone Filipino passenger. One of the Filipino crew said to me, "*Ikinararangal po namin na pasahero rin kayo* (We are proud that you are a passenger)". It made me wonder how they felt to be forced by economic realities in the Philippines to work in a service occupation and to be separated from their families for years. There were five young women in the crew. They said that they are treated fairly, but they worked long hours. It seems the Pinoys are well liked in the industry because they are efficient, hard workers, and docile. Deischa, the Pinay bartender, got a big tip from me at the end of the cruise because she learned to pour my usual drink quickly. The tour staff hung out at the bar and some nights I sang in the lounge while Michael, the staff pianist played. It's amazing how a little wine and distilled spirits could loosen the tongue. I heard intimate details of the staff's lives but I wasn't their psychiatrist, so I steered the topic away when they got serious. Analyzing personality psychodynamics without reimbursement wasn't in my plan!

But back to the passengers. We were a broad sample of tourists, mainly Caucasians from Canada, Australia, United Kingdom, Scotland, Belgium, a large tour group from Portugal, an Indian couple from Bombay, a Korean couple from Pasadena, and me. There were a lot of twenty-somethings in this group who were taking a break from life to find themselves by traveling all over South America for months with their backpacks and shoestring budgets. It was a splurge for them to be on this Antarctic cruise, much as it was for me. Some had quit school, others were in between jobs, and still others just didn't know what they wanted to do. Then there was the group of young couples who had jobs and mortgages but were traveling before the children arrived. There were hardly any in the middle ages, with very few in their 50's, and a large group of fit and able seniors in their 70's. The oldest was 81. I felt out of place, considering myself neither young nor senior, and I decide to throw my lot with the young ones for adventure.

There is a merry contingent of mostly young Portuguese tourists, thirty-some strong, and they take over the lounge every night and party. They come from all over Portugal, assembled by this travel agent who brought a TV crew to film their experience for travel marketing. They have a popular talk show host with them. She interviews the tour staff and ship crew, reports on what she's observing, and her cameraman is all over the place, practically stepping over the penguins. Some of the passengers are not fond of them. They do not mingle much as only a few speak English. I chat with a woman in the group who is a diplomat and who is serving as president of the UN Committee on Women's Rights. Her husband painstakingly harpoons each pea on his plate and sets them aside. He did not learn to eat his peas, I guess. The TV talk show host dares the Portuguese and anyone to jump into the freezing Antarctic. I take the dare. Loaded in two zodiacs, the ship's crew steered us derring-doers to a safe bank to catapult ourselves, and we dive, imagining that we are like the penguins sliding gracefully into the water. We are out as soon as we are in. The cold is numbing.

Shivering but exhilarated, we hurried back to the ship and saw in the distance a shelf of ice separate from the ice mountain in slow motion, and right before our eyes the wall of ice falls into the sea. We are mesmerized and stunned as we witness the calving. A crack cuts the stillness, a sharp fracture pierces our ears, and huge wave swells run toward us like a tsunami! And in a flash the ocean between us and the ship is littered with huge ice floes. Our zodiac can't maneuver through the ice litter. We have to wait for almost an hour until the ship repositions and makes a path for us to get through. It is the wrong moment for us to take that icy dip, but wait, the other zodiac is passing a hot thermos of brandy to us. The ship has a sauna and we warm up soon enough, before hypothermia sets in. All is well. The TV host interviews the divers later. I said that jumping in the frigid Antarctic is a triumph of recklessness but also courageous and liberating and that everyone should have it in his bucket list.

The Scot has the distinction of being the most flamboyant member of our group. He walks around indoors in his shorts, and in our zodiac landings, he comes down to the ice in his knickers and plaid kilt. I ask him if he wears any special garment under his skirt. "It shrinks," he told me. I wonder what he could have meant by that.

The Odd Couple are lovely people, but they stand out like Mutt and Jeff. The man must be 300 pounds and seven feet tall and the woman has the stigmata of an achondroplastic dwarf and barely passes the four foot mark. He is all flailing arms and legs while getting in and out of the zodiac, but he hasn't any idea how to do it. He contorts precariously to find footing on the boulders while taking pictures of the penguins. I thought he was going to crash into the rocks.

One time, he tries to be gallant by letting everybody climb into the zodiac first while he holds it steady, but mama mia, he is trying to put his legs first into the boat and standing instead of properly sitting on the side and easing inside. So the zodiac is unbalanced and he's there teetering on one leg and is about to fall so he catches himself and puts his foot wherever. And it is in a hole on the bow where the rubber connects to the rigid stepping platform and his leg is caught and he can't extricate it and he's stuck there, all 300 pounds sprawled and flailing. I am controlling myself from bursting into laughter. I am trembling into pieces. No one is laughing. I can't believe no one is reacting. This group of one-hundred and eight very different people is like that, very polite, very proper, very rule-abiding, very constipated! And his wife so sweetly says to him, "Dear, why don't you take out your foot from the boot? Here, I'll unlace your shoe.", and then she looks up to him lovingly, "Did you get a good shot of the penguins?". Everyone ignores the big spectacle, and it is so hilarious. My head is going to explode, so instead of laughing at the guy I burst out, "Shit!" And everyone cracks up.

Then there's the GP from Chicago who runs an addiction inpatient program, who takes notes at all the lectures and reviews them and underlines them later, and asks clarifying questions, then endlessly talks about the subject long after the session. Whew!

The Hostess is the name I've given to this lady who takes care of everyone at her table wherever she happens to sit for dinner, inquires about everyone, and includes everyone in the conversation. She is very accomplished in this task. She says all the proper things, she's impeccable. She has a retentive memory, and next day she greets you with your name. At trip's conclusion she seeks me out to say goodbye, reassures me that things will get better. She lost her husband nine years ago and now she is remarried for four years and happy again. She pries it out of me that I have a similar loss, when in fact I'd planned not to talk about it. She makes me cry, and it reminds me that I'm nowhere near things getting better. I'm still grieving.

So like the little red ship that has to reposition in the ice and set its course around the Great White Continent, I have to do the same. I have a lot in common after all with the young ones in this tour. They too are trying to find their position and are mapping the course of their journey.

The return trip seems endless. The Drake Passage crossing is real bumpy, and this time for a change, we round Cape Horn, and that is like being in a martini shaker. Everyone is battling nausea and goes to bed early. The fun is over.

We disembark in Ushuaia very early in the morning. I have until 2:30 pm until my flight back to Buenos Aires, then to the States. I book a 9 am tee time to play the golf course there. As I played the Juneau golf course in my Alaskan cruise, the northernmost golf course, I just have to play this golf course at the end of the world, 54 degrees, 29' 52" South Latitude. The Ushuaia Golf Club is a nine-hole course at the foot of the glacial mountain of Tierra del Fuego, along the river Pipo. The day is gorgeous. My first hole is a triple bogey but I finish with a par on ninth, and the score in between is of no concern.

CHAPTER 5: Fifty Shades of Light

Arctic Winter in Iceland

At 9 am it is pitch dark as the night. Imperceptibly, the contours of the landscape begin to develop like the slow appearance of images on photographic paper. The ghostly faint light takes on a fluorescent luminescence and is intensified by its reflection on the bright white snow. At 10 am the diffuse light concentrates in the southeast horizon and with backlighting effect, outlines the spilled milk splatter of clouds, and reveals the blue sky behind. The sun slowly peeks out of the horizon and throws off low-lying rays that fail to burst in exuberant energy. The rays are suspended in the sky in soft shades of pink, peach, and lemon yellow, with muted reds and oranges appearing in swatches between the clouds and where they meet the blue sky, magenta, lavender and eggplant shades and deep blues cool the rays further.

At 11 am the sun is just above the horizon and its rays shine on the earth. The ground is rendered featureless by snow, blanketing all in white the frozen lakes and rivers and mountains. There are no forests to break the white spread. The land, long denuded by glacial thaw, volcanic ash and man, has given up growing trees. Briefly the oblique slant of sunlight strikes against the obstacle of mountains. It rolls on the slope of the terrain, and it breaks into pigments, draping the landscape with a coat of many colors.

Before the sun can rise any higher, however, it begins to set, and dusk enters stealthily at 3 pm and the scene is illuminated as if by moonlight. At 4 pm night falls. Most days the fragmented clouds converge and block the sun completely. Light manifests as a frosted dome over the white landscape, white on white, obliterating landmarks, confounding perspective, and disorienting my sense of time. It is dusk all day, but there is no mistaking the night.

The aurora borealis will remain hidden during my entire visit. The magical transformation of energy into light, prompted by the collision of protons and electrons with the earth's magnetosphere, requires a cloudless sky. I am denied nature's magical and spectacular light show of dancing waterfalls and undulating curtains of green, purple, red, blues and all the rainbow hues in between.

CHAPTER 6: Out of Africa, Over the Rainbow

On our last day In Zanzibar, while sitting on a deck gently rocked by the lapping of waves, sipping our first cup of coffee, after an early morning beach walk to greet the sunrise, a spectacular rainbow swathed the sky and plunged into the horizon of the Indian Ocean. It was visible only for a brief moment, swallowed by the rising sun, but it added drama to our adventure in Africa, as we drew the final curtain. A stripe of many colors: a perfect image by which to capture my memories of these last two weeks.

My African Safari started in Nairobi. After a journey of 8,500 miles and an eighteen-hour flight from Atlanta via Amsterdam, I arrived at 8:30 pm of the next day, East Africa being seven hours ahead of EST. I had barely slept. I watched four movies en route, and had wine with the four meals I consumed. Furthermore, the wait for my luggage and visa processing was chaotic and very long. Jomo Kenyatta International Airport was basic and utilitarian, a stark departure from the gleaming and entertaining Schiphol, where many amusements were offered: a casino, trendy shops loaded with international goods, the Rijksmuseum which was featuring Jan Vermeer and his Girl with the Pearl Earrings. There were internet stations, restaurants, bars and coffee shops, sleek toilets and showers, a lounging area where you can stretch and snooze, a massage lounge, banks, currency exchange and ATM's. Looking around Jomo Kenyatta, it was spartan and drab by comparison.

I was exhausted as I took a taxi to my hotel, but less than five minutes on the road to the city center, the taxi headlight shone on a magnificent black and white striped horse that faced us from the street. A Zebra! It was so unexpected and so amazing that all fatigue left me, and I knew then that I was off to a great adventure.

Our experience of Kenya and Tanzania spanned over 2200 kilometers. We spent fourteen days trucking and camping from Nairobi to Dar es Salaam, and four days in Zanzibar. Driving to our destination was long and bumpy and dusty, and many places in our itinerary were not accessible by bus, train, or air. To experience the immense diversity that East Africa had to offer, we used a custom-fitted Mercedes overland truck that was a veritable hotel on wheels. The space under the seats was built with locked storage bins where we unpacked our luggage. The back-rests had shelves on them which stored groceries and dry foods and condiments. The truck had more shelves and storage underneath, and there it also housed the water tank, fuel tank, coal bin and the camp stools and tents. When we opened camp, the side panels went up and all things were on hand for making dinner. Peter, our Tanzanian tour assistant and cook, was amazing in the camp kitchen. Without a Cuisinart or an oven he prepared pureed soups, mashed peas and vegetables, and even baked a cake. Though he did the cooking and heavy cleaning, we all pitched in doing chores.

The trip I booked was midway between the really basic expedition and the luxury safari. I figured that the basic would be too rough and that the luxury option, aside from being very expensive, would not offer an authentic experience of the wilderness. We camped in organized campsites except for two nights spent in the wild, where there were absolutely no amenities. In organized campsites there were showers and toilets and electricity, and some had bars. A few had upgrades for basic lodging with an en suite bath which I took advantage of whenever offered. Camping got old very quickly.

One upgrade in the farm campsite in Kembu, was a charming 1 1/2 story cottage with a twin bedroom on the main level and a queen loft with a veranda and a kitchen. I shared this with two crazy guys from Vancouver. Our cook served tea rather than coffee, which I missed terribly, so it was a treat to have a kitchen where I brewed fresh Kenyan coffee for the three of us. In Mikadi, near Dar es Salaam, I upgraded to a palm-thatched beach hut. Here breaking waves lapped at my doorstep, sea breeze caressed me to sleep and the warm sunrise woke me up. In Kilimanjaro, I booked a cottage built in colonial times with extensive grounds planted with bougainvillea and hibiscus. From a large bar with cushioned couches to lounge in, I watched a bird keeper feed an orphaned falcon with raw meat.

It was a novelty for me to be camping and I didn't know what to expect. The first night, after driving down the escarpment of the Rift Valley, we pitched tent on the edge of Lake Naivasha. I laid awake listening to strange sounds and sensing the presence of living things outside my tent. I was told the next morning that hyenas and hippos were in the vicinity.

At the first camp I identified my travel buddies, and christened them, "The Truckin' Thrashers." They were a charming group of infantile men who needed a female audience to keep their excesses at scatological and lewd allusions in check. There was the monologist whose attention-seeking string was played endearingly by the artful picker and aided in mirthful harmony by the sidekick. The ensemble was completed by the passionate force of our man from Puglia. We sat around late into the night after everyone had zipped themselves into their sleeping bags. Cracking in mirth around the campfire or in the bar, we had been scolded about propriety and to mind our manners. The jokes and the laughs were all about the same things, intended to conquer sexual anxieties and homophobia and to titillate erotic fantasies. I smiled at them with indulgence even as I was tempted to wash their mouths with soap. In private, away from the guy group, they could be quite lovable men. I'll remember them fondly, for they made me feel special on this trip and the pleasure was mine.

Jambo! Karibu! Hello! Welcome! in Swahili. From Nairobi, we drove down to the Rift Valley on bumpy pot-holed roads. The shanty suburbs were teeming with activity of the market on Sunday. Kenya looked very poor. I was reminded of the squatter district in Tondo, Manila, and its dirt-floored huts, with corrugated aluminum roofs, and salvaged cardboard walls. Children waved and ran after the truck, laughing in merriment, and the people were very friendly. Everyone on the street saluted and greeted us. But tourism had corrupted some of them. In cities and touristy areas they were intrusive and accosted us with offerings of service or goods for sale. I got lost in the labyrinthine alleys of Zanzibar and I asked a little girl, about eleven or twelve years old, for directions. She asked for money first before showing me my way. Similarly, the taxi driver who took me to the Dar es Salaam airport quoted 15,000 shillings when I engaged him, a sum I verified clearly, and then tried to rip me off by demanding 50,000 when I got off. I prevailed.

The Rift Valley took my breath away. It was formed twenty million years ago by a violent tear of the Arabian and African tectonic plates and ripped the earth from Syria to Mozambique. In its wake volcanoes and lakes and mountains and vast plains were formed. The endless plains of the Serengeti, or siringit, as the Masai called it, was an ocean of undulating golden grass that stretched from horizon to horizon and beyond, as big as Belgium, as big as Ohio. Its surface was dotted by kopjes, charcoal-gray outcroppings of volcanic rock that took on fanciful shapes and precarious positions as they were molded by changing temperatures through the millennia. The immense landscape of grass was relieved by the graceful spreading crown of acacia trees.

It was the season of migration. Around January and February, 1.6 million wildebeests and hundreds of thousands of zebras, gazelles, impalas, topis, waterbucks, hartebeests, buffaloes, warthogs, and giraffes march from Masai Mara in Kenya to

Serengeti and Ngorongoro in Tanzania. They follow the rains to graze in the new vegetation and mate and give birth. Later in the year the reverse trip occurs as the rains turn north. It was dazzling to drive amongst these wild animals and see them up close and personal. There were wildebeests everywhere. They were massed in front of us and behind us and to each side. Against the horizon, thousands of them trudged along in a file, lined up nose to tail. They didn't bother us and we didn't bother them. They gave way for the truck to pass through.

We came upon a family of giraffes, lumbering, tall and colorful. They fed on acacia trees and sucked water from the tall cactus. Click and whirr, the cameras snapped. Zebras are marvels of evolution. To allow them to lower their heads to drink ground water, without having a fatal stroke from increased blood pressure to the head, their hearts evolved a system of valves to regulate blood flow. We camped in the wild and set out before the sun was up to look for the predators, to observe them as they stalked their prey and made their kills. With serendipitous timing, we spotted a lion as it was walking away after gorging on an impala. Two hyenas emerged from the bushes and helped themselves with the carcass. Meanwhile, vultures hovered in the vicinity, silent and patient. They perched vigilantly on nearby trees, ready to pounce as soon as the hyenas had had their fill. In a moment we heard shrieks and the rush of wings. About twenty vultures swooped into the abandoned remains in a feeding frenzy. In the distance the lion was walking away in a relaxed stride, looking for a cool spot under an acacia tree to rest and sleep. His hunger would be sated for the next three days.

Our guide spotted for us a solitary leopard up in a tree, and throughout our morning we saw jackals, hyenas, and more lions. In this wilderness we felt enlivened seeing a kill and other evidence of it with abandoned carcasses of downed wildebeests and antelopes, but in the backstreets of Zanzibar, we were repulsed and turned away from a cat feeding on its kill of an alley rat.

We drove next to Kenya to take a boat cruise on Lake Naivasha, one of the many lakes in the Rift Valley where hippos and birds could be easily spotted. We identified the fish eagle, ibis, and the kingfisher, as well as various sea gulls and pelicans, superb starlings, sparrows, an owl and a flock of the huge and strange bird, the marabou stork. Standing over five feet tall with a wingspan of more than ten feet, these African wading birds are scavengers of large carrion. They have featherless heads, grumpy faces and are so ugly they are cute. We visited Elsamere, the former home of Joy Adamson, of "Born Free" fame on the opposite bank of the lake. It was now a conservation center. We had tea on its lawn, where colobus monkeys stood alert and stole our crumpets, grinning playfully and making faces at us. In lake Nakuru, a soda lake, we beheld the dazzling sight of thousands of feeding flamingos, swathing the edge of the lake with a ribbon of pink. There were mean rhinos in the near distance, known to attack with the least provocation, and we had to walk behind the cover of the truck, to keep them at bay. We had lunch high on a kopje, and feasted on a sweeping panoramic view of all this grandeur. We spotted the rock hyrax, a tiny strange rodent-like animal that is the elephant's nearest relative, believe it or not, and we saw the elephants themselves. We saw herds of them, feeding on acacia trees and bulldozing the landscape.

We camped for a night on the banks of Lake Victoria, the second largest fresh water lake in the world. Next in size to Lake Superior, as big as Ireland, and bordered by Kenya, Tanzania, and Uganda, it holds the headwaters of the Nile. With a glass of wine we pondered the romance of its waters, flowing through the legendary river in the land of the Pharaohs, and we watched its spectacular sunset unfold before us.

We left Serengeti to drive to Ngorongoro, a collapsed crater 16 km wide and with steep walls 600 meters high. We camped at the rim of the crater before descending in five-man land-rovers early the next morning. As we opened camp three zebras galloped across our site, and as we tried to sleep hyenas laughed and kept us awake all night. But the night was magnificent, with a pitch black sky and brilliant constellations flanked by shooting stars that drew bright lines to the horizon. I was reminded of Van Gogh's swirling Starry Night.

We descended into the crater through the mist of early morning. The sunrise peeked out of the calderas rim and illuminated the lake below in muted and surreal light. The Masai men, who are allowed access to the Ngorongoro reserve, would lead his cattle from the village to the water every morning. Then he would doze in the shade and wait for every animal to finish grazing, and then finally herd them back to the village at night, to repeat the same thing next day. It seemed like a wonderful life, without a care in the world, until I remembered the life of the women. While the man was out dozing, the Masai women remained in the village and built their mud and dung huts, cooked, gathered wood, fetched water, and tended the children. Suddenly, the idea of living like a Masai seemed much less appetizing.

Ngorongoro was a natural zoo with about 100,000 animals living permanently there and swelling in numbers during migration. The elephant population was old and all male. The females stayed up above the caldera to remain with the children, as once in the bottom, they were not physically able to climb the steep walls of the crater. Similarly there were no giraffes, but everyone else was here. Land-rovers in huge numbers filled with tourists darted here and there in pursuit of animal specimens. In the Serengeti, where it was so vast, we seldom saw anyone else. Here, if a party spotted anything of interest it was relayed to the guides in other vehicles and everyone scrambled to the site. It was gridlock. It was unnatural and disconcerting, but it illustrated the dilemma that tourism poses in this country. It is a poor country and needs dollar exchange revenue badly. It has limited habitable land, and population that is growing fast, yet they have reserved vast wild parklands for the rest of the world to experience. There is no place on earth quite like this.

We paused at the hippo pool for lunch and we were warned to guard our meal from the black kites, scavenger birds who had learned to steal the lunches of tourists. I had barely lowered myself to sit on a piece of driftwood under a tree when a kite swooped from nowhere and ripped the two sandwich bags from my hands, nearly amputating my fingers. "Shit," I cried, "there goes my lunch!" I was still fuming as I told the story later when something dropped at my feet. It was one of the bags, with a piece of bread crust still in it. I looked up to where it had come from and over my head, up there in the tree, was the bird, amused at my expense. And then I felt something trickling down my legs. Chalky guano, bird excrement! Such nerve! I got no respect in Ngongoro.

It was a long drive to Kilimanjaro but I was filled with anticipation. I recalled Hemingway's "Snows of Kilimanjaro", and the movie with Gregory Peck and Susan Hayward and Ava Gardner. I saw it as an adolescent in the Philippines, and I fell in love with it! I had yearnings even then to go to Africa and to see the world, and here I was, right in its bosom. I had to climb Kili. It was the highest free-standing mountain in the world at 19335 ft (5895 m), rising from the hot savannah and rolling plains of the Great Rift Valley to a frigid, snow-covered peak. One could climb it without mountaineering skills but one had to be fit and withstand sustained running for half an hour. The altitude could be a killer.

It took four hours of hiking to reach Mandara base camp from the Kilimanjaro Marangu Park Gate on the bottom slope. I was huffing and puffing and stopped every twenty steps for the last thirty minutes to catch my breath. *Pole-pole,* "slowly," in Swahili, was how you finished. I never acclimatized to the low oxygen tension, climbing only to 2700 m to reach the Mandara base camp. I would not climb Kili to its snow-capped peak after all. The descent, however, was a cinch. There was a refreshing drizzle, and as breathing got easier, I took in the beauty of the tropical lushness along the way.

After ten days of camping we were weary and ready to relax on the beach of Zanzibar. The drive was long and wound through sisal, coffee and tea plantations before descending to sea level and confronting the heat and humidity.

We reached the port of Dar es Salaam, a busy city teeming with people and honking vehicles. Until now, we had encountered only occasional trucks and buses on the road. There were no private cars on the highway in Africa. The locals walked to their destinations, sometimes across long distances and on bare feet. From Dar we took a two-hour ferry ride to cross the channel to Zanzibar. The ferry was packed. There were custom checks and bag inspections. The locals elbowed their way through and did not queue, and I was starting to get a headache from the stink of body odor. I had to cover my knees and arms in deference to the majority Muslim population, and I was soaked with sweat. We were held in an airless packed compartment, six to a row, and we were told that the sailing was more choppy than usual. I needed to breathe. I got out of my seat and stood on the deck among the crates and sacks and chickens in cages. Sa'id, the ticket conductor, invited me to the bow of the ferry where there was a better view and where I could sit on a stair and face the horizon. I remembered my grandfather, who was a fisherman, "To avoid getting seasick, face the horizon," a lifelong lesson which made me seaworthy. On the way to the bow, I had to pass through the galley and I got to meet the captain and the officers. Captain

Chile was chatty, and we had a long conversation. He informed me that Coretta King had died.

There are no more gigolos on the beaches of Zanzibar. That went with the Aga Khan and Rita Hayworth. Zanzibar is steeped in exotic and ignominious history. In its heyday, it was a busy and rich trading post for cloves and other spices, ivory and slaves. It was ruled by sultans and sheiks who lived in gilded palaces. It was a tropical island with bananas and coconut trees, fine white sand beaches and the red colobus monkey. But now it was run down and faded like an old dowager who had lost her fortune. It was slowly crumbling into decay. Many sections were in ruins with the dwelling's guts exposed and inhabited by alley cats. It had become receptacles for the ubiquitous used plastic bags that littered everywhere. But even under the dilapidation, I could imagine how it could be a jewel if restored and cared for. Stone Town, with its narrow alleys and remains of grand houses with intricately carved doors and brass finials, suggests a past that was magnificent and shining.

The oceanside park was inhabited by locals who squatted or napped there all day. I was aggressively pursued with touts of tours or goods or taxi for hire. At night it was lovely from a distance with the night fish market and bazaar, but it was intimidating for the tourist to stroll through. There was a program unveiled for restoration, but the government has no money and has no private benefactors to do the massive work. It is such a pity for a world heritage site. There was, however, a Freddie Mercury restaurant. There were several other fine restaurants housed in the few restored grand houses, and the meals were cheap and the South African wines were great, as well as the beers, Kilimanjaro and Tusker. I tried a Chinese restaurant, and it felt strange not to have pork on the menu. The newly appointed Minister of Agriculture was being honored at the next table. There was a nice shopping section but there were no unique bling to buy. Tanzania was not the place to buy Tanzanite jewelry. There were no chic shops. In New York and Las Vegas I saw the best designs in Tanzanite. In Stone Town, the old slave market could be visited, and in Prison Island, recalcitrant slaves were held until shipped to the New World.

To cap our safari, we went to the beach in Nungwi, which was north of the island and one and a half hours from Stone Town. It took some determination. The road was dusty and bumpy and ridden with pot-holes, passing through little villages of thatched huts and roadside vegetable stands. In Nungwi Village our accommodations were third rate but adequate. Nearby, a twenty minute walk on the beach, was a new international caliber resort, Gemma del Est, with competitive international 5-star rates, but expensive by local standards. Regardless of where one stayed, the beach was the picture of paradise. There were endless and broad stretches of fine white sand, turquoise waters, clear blue skies, coconut trees curtsying to the sand, and quiet coves where there was nobody but me. I spent the day following a snail as it crossed a sand ripple. I watched a spindly sea urchin roll on its many spines, studied shallow pools formed by the receding tide, turned over stones to coax colorful fish out in the open, picked shells, and stalked crabs. I read a book, dozing and dreaming, and was refreshed by the gentle breeze and the rhythmic lapping of the waves.

I arrived at Hartsfield-Jackson in a downpour and learned that my sister was boycotting her daughter's wedding, that my son and his girlfriend had broken up, that my Philippine Foundation executive director had resigned, and that Coretta King was dead. I was back to my life, but on that last day in Zanzibar the rainbow dipped into the horizon and I dreamed that I could find the other end in the Amazon.

CHAPTER 7: Ich Liebe Berlin

Berlin is a city emerging from the rubble of bombings, and is trying to come to terms with and move on from its dark and ignominious past. The city has grand boulevards and majestic roundabouts, and the sprawling central park of Tiergarten. This was the hunting ground of past royalty, and now it is just lovely covered in fresh snow, the same weather which has dumped tons in the rest of Europe and paralyzed transportation.

Doobie and I took the double-decker bus hop on and off city tour while it was snowing, which rendered the city views pristine and brilliant until the afternoon when it became heavy and dark. I was cozy in my ankle-length mink. I had hesitated to bring it at first, but now I felt that I'd made a wise decision. I bought a wool cloche, loathing the Euro price since I knew I could get a similar one from Loehmann's at 75% off, but I needed a hat in the snow. I left it on the bus at our first stop, then Doobie and I got separated and went on with the tour independently. I hopped back on the bus at Checkpoint Charlie about two hours later and I couldn't believe it! There was my cloche on an empty seat. I felt it was my lucky day. Checkpoint Charlie was the border crossing between East and West Berlin when the Wall stood from August 1961 to November 9,1989. Berlin has been divided and reunited many times, parceled out among various nations as war booty and divided into four sectors at one point. There were whole neighborhood sections that had been bombed to smithereens during WWII. Despite the city being 750 years old, I could scarcely spot any old buildings. But the government was reconstructing it as it was, and heavy equipment and lorries were everywhere, digging up the rubble and building anew. There were sections that were completely modern, marked with distinctive architecture designed by important international architects, such as in the Potsdamerplatz, the equivalent of Times Square and in the superlative Friedrichstrasse shopping arcades. The Kurfurstendamm, or Ku'damm for short, is the longest street in Berlin and is very charming and romantic with double sidewalks lined with cafes and shops and with trees and park seats in the center promenade. Bismarck, who I think felt culturally inferior, designed this after the Champs-Élysées and captured its splendor.

The rebuilt Reichstag, the seat of the Republic, has a new observation dome atop it, with its intricate mirror panels and a spiraling ramp where I could stroll and have a panoramic view of the entire city. It is a work of art built by an important London architect. Not far is the historic Brandenburg Tor, where part of the Wall once stood, and south of it is the newly opened Holocaust Memorial designed by American architect Eisenmann. It is a field of 2711 concrete stelae in a grid pattern, each varying in height, covering a whole city block. It produces an undulating and seemingly unstable surface if viewed as a whole composition. Along the shorter pillars of the field it suggests rows of perfectly lined coffins as far as the eye can see. I walked in between the stelae and found my way among the pillars. Among the tallest ones I felt an oppressive feeling, as if the walls were closing in. Underground is the Holocaust Museum, a place so gripping I broke down in tears. I emerged very angry at Bush's policies, for many of them were reminiscent of Hitler's initial political moves. We stayed at the Westin Grand on Friedrichstrasse, a former palace which was decked to the hilt in Christmas lights and holiday trimmings. It has a central six-story foyer with a stained glass domed ceiling and a grand staircase where carolers lined up to entertain guests. Berlin is big on the holidays, just like it's big on its mascot, the Berlin bear, which was in effigy or looming as a sculpture in corners and sidewalks all over town.

Christmas bazaars and fairs were popping up in every neighborhood and at major commercial intersections. We

45

checked out the bazaar near our hotel, in the Forum on Unter den Linden, a square flanked with beautiful buildings like the Staatsoper and St. Hedwig Cathedral. I stopped for a moment at St. Hedwig and paid my respects. It is an odd Catholic church, with no central space or nave, and the main church space is in the basement level and divided into several chapels. These Christmas bazaars are so nostalgic and festive. They are clustered wooden booths dressed with holiday lights and glitter. They sold crafts and the usual imported doodads from developing countries, and gifts and holiday decorations. Food concessions with bratwurst stands and cheese and spun sugar candies, fried dough breads, pastries and chocolates were to die for.

In the Thai booth I sampled their noodles, then proceeded to the cappuccinos, hot chocolates and warm spiced wine laced with amaretto.

The bigger bazaars came with old-fashioned fairs with Ferris wheels and carousels and music grinders with hustling monkeys (now robotized). I mingled with the German populace, and as a group they are a handsome lot after the Scandinavians. They are rule abiding. They stand at the street corner waiting for the green pedestrian light, they don't cross even if they've been standing for ages and there isn't any car in sight. The rule goes both ways. They don't stop for jaywalking pedestrians, and would run over you if you cross on the red light. The food is robust and sticks to your bones, made the old-fashion way with real butter and fat on the meat. We dined in various restaurants and cafes along the River Spree. Maya, my niece who lived there, took us to her favorite cafe where we had desserts and coffee and played mahjong for one jai-alai, which Dobbs won. Maya requested a mahjong set for my *pasalubong* (hostess gift), and she wanted to play right away so she could refresh her memory of the game. She planned to introduce the game to her friends.

In one café, they had a ticker tape of the beer prices on view on TV screens so we could check how much our favorite beer was going by the glass. I sampled the traditional holiday menu of goose, venison, and duck, and various sausages. We drank only beer, sampling lagers and pilsners, dark and wheat beer as much as we could. I gained three pounds. We took two trains on the U-bahn to get to Maya's flat for coffee and cakes in the mixed section of the city. Heretofore we hadn't met any ethnics or colored, except ourselves. Here, most of the ethnics are Turks, and their story as minorities is the same as minorities in America. We met two of Maya's roommates, Ian and Karen. Maya's building was a cooperative, and they were in the midst of renovating and painting in their individual units. The roommates all had interesting resumes. Ian was a set designer and carpenter and built his bed platform himself, which was very funky in black, and original and funkier still, his shelves were stacked steel laundry drums which worked very well for storing his clothing. Maya's space had tall windows which she draped in sheer gossamer, and she had good light to keep her tropical indoor plants in good health.

At the flat, we had melt-in-your mouth cakes in different flavors, with various berry fillings and chocolate and cream layers from Maya's favorite bakery, and washed them down with coffee. Karen spread a blue cloth on the dining table and arranged in the center votive candles and yellow autumn leaves she'd picked from the courtyard below. We had lively conversation about the state of the world, why the holocaust happened, the minority issue in Germany and in America, the state of our schools, the unemployment in Germany and the European Union, about the job-nomads (my new favorite term) and entertainment junkies among the X-generation, and time just flew. I was almost late for La Boheme at 7 pm at the Komische opera. Maya and Doobs had their own schedule to cruise the bars and check the rock and roll bands until 3 am. I was miserable after the opera, with a cough and a headache. I didn't feel like having dinner, and I had to beg for aspirin from the concierge. I had potato and sausage soup in the lobby and a wheat beer, packed, scheduled a wake-up call at 4 am and went to bed. Our return flight was at 7:10 am.

CHAPTER 8: Bonjour Paris! Pour Deux S'il Vous Plait

We had been in Paris for less than forty-eight hours before we got yelled at and called, "fucking bitches!" by this deli chef in the neighborhood of Passy in the 16th arrondisement, where we'd rented a one-bedroom apartment for our pied-à-terre in this lively ville de lumières.

It was on our second day after arrival, a Sunday. We slept late, catching up with the six-hour jet lag and the four-hour flight delay from the States. Evelyn wanted to go to church, but all the masses in our neighborhood were over after 12:30 pm, so we decided to start our sightseeing in Sacre Coeur and hopefully catch a mass there.

We bought a discounted packet of ten metro subway tickets and used them to get to the Abbesses stop for what we thought would be short walk to Sacre Coeur. We got off the train and ascended over thirty meters of endless steps winding around and around a colorful stairwell of tile mosaic and painted walls and art nouveau lighting fixtures. We emerged on Montmarte panting and with tachycardia, through an art deco bronze and cast iron gate, just one of two remaining original Paris metro entrances designed by famed architect Hector Guimard. Well, that was ahh, robust and really breathtaking. We didn't know there was an elevator. We walked to a bustling and festive street scene, with playing children, street musicians, and a carousel on the street corner. Bistros and cafes and shops lined the narrow cobblestone alleys and the bright sun warmed the cool air. Brilliant light fell on the red and pink geraniums of balcony gardens, and we were filled with excitement. This was how we imagined our Paris visit would be.

We sat al fresco at Cafe Consulat and had a marvelous lunch and a glass of wine. Climbing steps again to the Montmarte butte, where the resplendent Basilica of the Sacred Heart stood majestically over Paris, we passed the last remaining wooden windmill of Montmarte and the smaller cemetery of St. Vincent. We were lucky to catch a mass at 4 pm, and so we felt fulfilled in our obligations. We took the funicular down to Pigalle just for the fun of it, cruised the souvenir shops, and because of Evelyn's objections I passed on checking the sex shops for toys and passed on the Moulin Rouge Cancan Revue. She also declined to dine in the Pigalle area, so we took the Metro back to Passy and since it was very late, we decided to just stop by the Deli Cafe a block from the metro station for carry out.

The deli chef was charming and bantered with us, showing off his English and asking where we were from. He joked around some, and we even thought that he was flirting. Then he started adding up our purchases in French and we couldn't keep up with the numbers, so we requested a printed receipt. He said his cash register wasn't working right, so he couldn't do it, then he wouldn't accept a credit card. When we pressed, he said our card wasn't going through, but he was swiping it wrong. We showed him how, and we asked him again to review our purchases for accuracy. There he got all bent out of shape, became agitated, and accused us of calling him a liar. I told him to stop and focus on completing our purchase. He got all excited about the credit card not going through so I said, "OK, just get this over with and I'll give you cash but listen, I'm very displeased, but let's go ahead with the purchase." He yelled that we could take our business somewhere else, and started to say something about Philippine women. "Don't go there," I told him. "Just shut up and finish." That's when he went into apoplexy and called us the b-name for everyone in the café to hear. We got our food and told him he just lost two customers, and I decided not to give him the finger. We left quickly and said no more.

Evelyn and I had planned this trip last year after reminiscing about Julma, our high school classmate from Colegio de Santa Isabel in Naga City, who became a nun. Evelyn, Noy and I had developed a tradition after Johnny died, of spending the time around my birthday at Evelyn's lakeside home in Michigan. We googled her one time, and found out that she was the General Councillor of her Congregation, the first Asian to be elected to that position. Before her election to their General Council, she was Provincial of her congregation in The Philippines. In that capacity, she also served as Chairperson of the Association of Major Superiors of Women Religious in The Philippines. She had assisted her religious order as a writer, speaker and resource person. Before her investiture in the order she was a TOYM (Ten Outstanding Young Men/Women) awardee.

We learned that she was in Paris in the mother house of the Sisters of Charity of St. Vincent de Paul. Sr. I wrote her at the Rue du Bac address. She e-mailed back promptly, excited to hear from us. Her calendar was very full and we managed to find mutually available dates for August, but when our trip finally came together for the week of August 25-September 1, she was suddenly called to go to Indonesia, leaving only August 25, my birthday, available for our visit. Noy could not make it as she had been in a car accident which disabled her for months and consumed all her leave days. Evelyn, who suffered flying phobia, had to steel herself to make this trip. Having a reunion with Julma after forty-eight years motivated her though and she distinguished herself admirably on the plane. At the end of it, the Lady of rue du Bac proved her miraculous powers. Evelyn was cured of her flying phobia and promptly made plans to fly for her next trip.

Our US flight was four hours late of its 8:24 am arrival at CDG, and Julma had checked on our arrival twice already, so our gardienne, the apartment landlady, informed us. She was apparently waiting to have lunch with us. So we put our bags down, and without changing our travel clothes, we took the metro to Sevres Babylone and crossed the street to 140 rue du Bac, and there was Julma and us all choked up. We'd left each other as girls in 1959, and were meeting again for the first time across oceans and continents and time.

In this chapel of the Convent of the Filles de la Charité, La Chapelle Notre-Dame de la Médaille Miraculeuse 140, rue du Bac, the Holy Virgin appeared to Catherine Laboure on the 18th of July 1830. Catherine Labouré was at that time preparing herself to become a sister. On the 28th of November, the Holy Virgin entrusted Catherine with the miraculous medal and this gave birth to a new devotion to the Blessed Virgin. Today, two millions pilgrims visit the chapel each year. Fervent celebrations are held every day, and this chapel is the second-most popular pilgrimage in France after Lourdes. Since the time of Catherine's death, two billion miraculous medals had been distributed

We walked in the convent's bright, tranquil gardens. Julma introduced us to her colleagues, all very touched and happy for our remarkable reunion. We toured the conference facilities and the public quarters. She talked about the challenges of dwindling religious postulants, her work in Southeast Asia, her experiences in Paris, and her wish to return and do work in the Philippines. We observed her attitude of obedience and service, her calm and serenity, her open-mindedness and lack of proselytizing, and I marveled. I envied her fluency in French, whereas I've struggled with learning Spanish for years. She took us around the convent's neighborhood, among its streets and alleys. We looked for a place to have a late lunch, and we ended up in a Vietnamese fast food place where we lingered over coffee until we couldn't keep our eyes open any longer, and had to go. We stopped at Bon Marche food section to purchase takeout food for dinner, and threw in a bottle of wine and some cheese and pastries for breakfast. It was great to see Julma. It felt like we'd always been together, like we'd just picked up where we left off. I told her I cried and I was confused when I learned she entered the nunnery. I told her that I'd felt sorry for her, and that I thought the sisters had brainwashed her. Why be a nun when we both knew there were so many young men who'd had crushes on her? I knew, of course, that she'd given this deep thought and that she was very learned about her catholic religion and she had actively chosen this life. She had the elusive thing that I couldn't grasp, and that was faith.

Julma left for Indonesia, and Evelyn and I were on our own in Paris. This was my fourth trip to Paris, so I was familiar with most of the tourist sites, but I had others in charge of my prior tours. Evelyn was counting on me to have a memorable trip. We decided to take the hop-on, hop-off tourist water-bus to see the sights, as it offered a unique view of Paris from the Seine. It was super, it did not have to contend with traffic and the noise and heat of concrete and exhaust fumes. It would have been a perfect day to explore the Musee d'Orsay, but it was closed on Mondays. We explored Notre Dame and the Latin quarter, St. Germain des Pres, the Hotel de Ville, which is the seat of the City municipal government and the nearby le Marais, emerging as the trendsetter of Paris chic and urbanity. We also took a tour of all the best bridges: Pont Alexander, Pont Neuf, Pont Royal, Pont des Arts, Pont de la Concorde, and the bridge to Passy where our apartment was, Bir Hakiem.

We got off at the Louvre and went under the glass pyramid to check out the mall and the restaurants. We skipped visiting the art galleries because we didn't have the time, and reserved this for a more leisurely visit. Instead we shopped the museum mall for souvenirs. I bought three children's books and a pair of medieval masks which I forgot on the bench at the Louvre water-bus stop. We strolled the nearby Tuileries gardens and found a shaded bench from which to watch people and rest our feet. The water-bus terminus is at the foot of the Eiffel tower, so we put this last on our tour and planned to have dinner at the tower platform in the Jules Verne Restaurant, but alas, it was closed for renovations. We stopped by a bistro in the Grenelle neighborhood. On the way home, as we crossed the bridge to the right bank of the Seine, the Eiffel tower stood against the night sky, bathed in golden light. In the train every night as it crossed the Bir Hakiem bridge we watched the Eiffel emerge from the tree tops, and if the time was right we caught it covered with twinkling lights dancing all over its surface. I caught it one night alongside the moon, and took a great photo.

We wanted a taste of Paris shopping so on the fourth day we took the metro to the Opera, and started on Haussman Boulevard. We checked out the Galleries Lafayette and Printemps, then took a breather at Cafe La Paix for lunch. We then proceeded to Place Vendome and checked out all the mouth-watering baubles at Cartier, Van Cleef and Arpels, Boucheron, and the like. We were covetous browsing on rue St Honoré, the boulevard Capucine and rue Royal. We splurged on Louis Vuitton presents. We went home excited with our purchases and wanted to deposit them before going out for dinner in a fancy restaurant. By this time we were getting tired of bistro menu, and we wanted something real nice, like grilled fresh foie gras or côte de veau.

But then, horror! We forgot our key inside the apartment! We got into the ante foyer by using the code at the door 3436B, which we remembered by thinking of bra sizes which did not fit us, and we got to the inside foyer through a resident who happened to arrive. The gardienne, Lydia, was the homebody sort who was always around, but she wasn't there now. After waiting over an hour, Danielle, who had been a resident for twenty-five years and who knew Lydia, arrived and knew that Lydia was babysitting for a friend that night. She had, however, her phone number. Lydia arrived all flustered to discover that she left her keys in her apartment too! Mon Dieu! But not to worry, her son lived upstairs and had a key to her apartment. That did the trick. We all got in and found our keys where we left them, on the mantle. By this time, it was too late to eat anywhere but we found a Chinese buffet in Passy, about to close for the night, but we persuaded the owner to let us have the remaining scraps.

The next day we took the RER train for a day of designer outlet shopping in La Vallee Village, thirty-five minutes east of Paris. We got off one stop before Disneyland Paris, at Val d'Europe. We learned the hard way that the Paris metro tickets were not good for the suburban RER trains. The exit turnstile wouldn't open for us until we paid the supplement price of Eu4.50. I didn't get too excited in these outlet stores, as I could get better deals at Loehmann's and at Sak's and Parisian when they held their super discount sales.

Everybody goes to Versailles when they visit Paris. We took another RER to travel twenty-five minutes southwest of Paris. It was a beautiful day, and we took our time, lingered in the gardens, and took long walks to the Grand Trianon and the Petit Trianon and to Marie Antionette's hamlet, the jardin anglaise where the grand queen once played country maid. We had a delightful lunch at the La Petite Venise, a wonderfully conceived restaurant in the old boat house that once housed the King's Venetian gondoliers and oarsmen.

All this touring was beginning to wear us out. We were just about to settle in for a quiet day of reading or watching TV, but we discovered that all of the TV channels was in French, and that the apartment did not have enough good light for reading. We'd been losing sleep because this charming apartment with its high ceilings and lovely embossed ceiling trays, herringbone-patterned wood floors, antique furnishings, and art on the walls, had no sound insulation at all. In fact, the walls acted like conductors of the feeblest sound from elsewhere in the building. We could hear footfalls above, the rustling of paper, conversations, the rush of water in the pipes, the roar of flushing toilets, and the heavy metal clang of the iron elevator outside our door. Lydia bustled noisily in the courtyard every morning, dragging out garbage bins and hosing them down until they sounded like marching-band drums. But she was a dear otherwise, very helpful and friendly. She arranged our airport shuttle and gave us tips and directions. We gave her a bottle of Bordeaux in appreciation.

On our last day we took the metro to Etoile and visited the arc d'triomphe, then walked down Champs Elysee to the Place de Concorde. We hunted down the restored art deco covered shopping arcades and galleries, which were popular Parisian hangouts at the turn of the century and the prototype of the modern shopping malls. Along the vicinity of Palais Royal and Rue St Denis we stumbled on Passage Jouffroy , Choisuel, and de Perron. These were in various stages of restoration, and very charming with mosaic tiled floors, wood paneling store fronts and glass domed ceilings. We meandered along the Grand Boulevards; des Italiens, des Capucines, and Rue Royal. We rested our feet as we watched a dance performance on the square at Place Colette. We found ourselves on Boulevard Montmarte and was amazed at the distance we'd covered. We had dinner in a fancy restaurant and went back to Passy to pack. We didn't have any problem getting our VAT refund at the airport and the flight back was almost on time, just half an hour late, and customs was a breeze. After all we didn't bring in any Frenchman! A bientôt, Paris!.

CHAPTER 9: The Lost World, Romance of Travel

I remember the first time I yearned to see the world, back in World History class in high school. Epochs and kingdoms and exotic names and distant peoples and places came alive in my imagination, and a deep longing took hold within me to walk the earth and breathe the air of these magical lands. The Pharaohs, Antony and Cleopatra, Mesopotamia, Babylon, Baghdad, Damascus, Constantinople, Nebuchadnezzar, King David, Solomon, the Ottoman Empire, Richard the Lion Hearted, Saladin; their stories conjured narratives in my head more thrilling than what Hollywood has ever created. So it is with great anticipation that I planned this trip to Israel, Egypt and Jordan.

Last year I signed up as a volunteer in a weeklong English immersion program for Spaniards, Pueblo Ingles, in La Alberca and met Talila, who was from Israel, and who assured me that visiting Israel is not as scary as what the US media portrays it to be. I've wanted to go for the last fifteen years, but was daunted by the perennial State Department travel advisory to this region. I feared that the lands that I'd imagined might be lost forever to the local wars and terrorism. Baghdad, Damascus, Persia (Iran), and Lebanon have all been defiled by violence, and the Arab lands of Saudi Arabia, Dubai Abu Dhabi, and Qatar have been altered beyond recognition by glitzy development of skyscrapers, mega-cities, mega-malls and golf courses. So I decided that it was then or never, and that I would go!

I must admit, I had some trepidation, and the fearful concern of friends didn't help, so I purchased an expensive travel insurance that included terrorism coverage. My trip was without incident, however, except for the medical challenge of subduing a virulent staphylococcus colony that grew from a yellow jacket sting on my right calf that I got while playing golf before leaving.

I flew into Tel Aviv's Ben Gurion airport from JFK in New York after a 12-hour flight, arriving the next day since Israel is ahead 6 hours of EST. A friend informed me that I would be questioned in JFK about my purpose for traveling to Israel and other details of my itinerary, but none of this happened during both departure and arrival. Ben Gurion immigration check was a breeze. The airport is sleek and modern, everything was easy to navigate, and there were no uniformed soldiers in sight. I arrived on the eve of Passover, so the flight was full of Jewish families going home for the holidays. I did, however, have a strange feeling of "otherness". I looked different from the crowd, and then I noticed that people were behaving differently, too. The men wore their skullcaps or yarmulkas and their tallits, prayer shawls. Men and women were reading from the Torah throughout the trip and every so often the men would stand on the aisle and pray from the Torah. I sat next to a young man, Ariel, who imports mid-priced fashion from China and the US into Israel. He's orthodox Jew. He pitched the wonders of the homeland and the self-affirmation of living in Israel, and expressed regret that his lifestyle as an entrepreneur prevents him from dedicating his life to the study of the Torah full time. When I told him that I was invited to a Seder in my friend's kibbutz, he educated me about the holiday and gave me pointers about etiquette and customs. I purchased a Kosher gift basket from the duty free shops on arrival.

The sensation of "otherness" was something I felt throughout my entire trip. Kosher rules are observed in all places, including major hotels. Pork, mollusk, and shellfish are not served. As it was the Passover, neither beer nor bread were served during our meals. On the Shabbat, there were no hot meals and the elevator was on auto-pilot, stopping on every floor. Business closed at 2 pm on Friday and didn't reopen until sundown on Saturday, buses did not run. I wanted to fly out to Cairo from Tel Aviv on Friday, but I had to take a 12:40 am departure as there was no flight scheduled until Sunday. I couldn't get a doctor to evaluate my leg cellulitis until past 2 pm on Friday, and by that time I couldn't get my antibiotic prescription filled except in the Christian Arab section of Old Jerusalem. In Old Jerusalem, Orthodox, Hasidic, Ashkenazi, and Sephardic Jewish men wear their traditional clothing, and it felt like I was in a time warp. I contemplated in silence in front of the Western (Wailing) Wall, the holiest Jewish site, and was very cognizant of the separate men's and women's sections. According to tradition, I inserted a small slip of paper in the stone crack where I wrote down my fervent wishes. The devout are very emotional at the wall, kissing and stroking the stone, crying, murmuring or transfixed in reverence. In August 2003 a Palestinian suicide bomber detonated in a bus carrying worshippers from the wall killing twenty and injuring many including children. Now there's a checkpoint and metal detector at the entrance to the Wall plaza.

In Egypt and Jordan, being Muslim countries, the hijab, modest dressing for men and women, is most striking among the women, who wear long loose-fitting clothing and scarves that cover everything except the face and hands. Its extreme practice is exemplified by women from Iran and Saudi Arabia, which observe Sharia law. There, they wear the burqa, black costume with complete body and face cover, leaving only small slits for the eyes. The men wear turbans and distinctive head gears and the loose fitting galabiyya. I was at an Arab restaurant and I couldn't help staring at one of these burqa-clad women, to see how they ate. It seemed very difficult to me as I watched them pass food under the veil. I briefly contemplated how these women could enjoy fast food. Kentucky Fried Chicken, McDonald's, Pizza Hut, and Starbucks were everywhere to be found, but the obstacles posed by the veil seemed to render moot the simple pleasures of finger-food. How could they ever eat fried chicken and enjoy it? The Muslims are not allowed to drink, so I was not able to enjoy my meals with wine.

I was enthralled by the idea of following the biblical events in these three countries, beginning with the exodus, where Moses led the Israelites from slavery in Egypt to the promised land, through the desert and mountains and the Red Sea. The Passover Seder with my friend in her kibbutz was particularly moving with its ceremony and symbolism. In Jordan, you can actually step on the same ground Moses traveled in Mt. Nebo, where he received the Ten Commandments, and from this perch, viewed the Promised Land and the Garden of Eden. I filled a plastic bottle of water from the Jordan River, where St. John the Baptist baptized Jesus Christ. In Jerusalem on Good Friday, I meditated in the Garden of Getshemane, in the Mount of Olives, where the Church of All Nations (Basilica of the Agony), Mary Magdalene's Church, and the Dominus Flevit Church stand. In the afternoon I followed Jesus' journey of the cross in the Via Dolorosa, the first nine stations winding through the narrow and bustling alleys of the Arab bazaars in Old Jerusalem, and the last five in Golgotha. On the hill of Calvary sits the Basilica of the Holy Sepulcher, a complex of several churches joined together and controlled by various religious communities, the three major ones being the Franciscan Order of the Roman Catholics, the Greek Orthodox and the Armenian Apostolic Churches. The 11th station site, where Jesus was nailed to the cross, is guarded by Roman Catholics, whereas on the spot where Jesus' cross and the crosses of the two criminals were raised on Mt. Calvary is now a Greek Orthodox altar. The tomb, carved from rock and encased in marble, is in the main rotunda below the magnificent central dome of the basilica and within a small chapel. There is always a long line to enter the chapel and view the tomb. The various religious communities owning parts of the basilica are far from models of tolerance and peace. For centuries, they have squabbled over property rights to the point of violence and have never found a resolution beyond the status quo agreement forged centuries ago. A wooden ladder had stood on the front window ledge since the 19th century and remains to this day and since the area is common ground, nobody dares to touch the ladder for fear of retribution from the others

On Easter Sunday we braved crossing the security checkpoints to visit Bethlehem in the Palestinian territory. We learned that there are three levels of political authority in these areas: Israeli, Palestinian, and combined jurisdiction. It is relatively safe for tourists to go to Bethlehem, which needs tourist currency, but it is dangerous for Israelis because of the potential for kidnapping. Attacks from terrorists have declined since the building of the border wall and instituting checkpoints, but nevertheless our tour guide took some cloak-and-dagger precautions. At the Israeli checkpoint she sat in the back of the bus and instructed us to declare her a fellow tourist if questioned, and at the Palestinian checkpoint she got picked up by Palestinian Arab conspirators while we went through passport checks. We were taken in another vehicle after the border check, and our tour guide joined us later.

Despite the excitement of this adventure, the outcome was uneventful, and I had only to deal with some hard questioning from the Israeli police. I was transporting a big box, which concerned them, but it contained only the finely carved olive wood nativity set by Zacharia Bros., that I'd purchased to add to my creche collection.

The Basilica of the Nativity is one of the oldest continuously used churches in the world and is actually two churches joined together. The bigger one is Greek Orthodox and the other, St. Catherine's, is Catholic. It is built over the grotto where Jesus was believed to have been born. I queued to view the underground cave where tourists jostled for entrance, and the guards did not impose order but took requests from some tour guides to let their clients in with priority. I later learned that money changed hands to earn this privilege. Again, as in the Church of the Holy Sepulcher, the various religious communities guarding this holy site have a status quo arrangement that has been maintained since centuries ago.

On the way to Ein Gev, a kibbutz resort on the eastern shore of the Sea of Galilee, we passed Tiberias and Meggido, the site where Armageddon is prophesied to take place. I strolled on the banks of the Sea of Galilee, in reality a lake fed by the Jordan river and underwater springs. It is the lowest freshwater lake in the world, second only to the salinated Dead Sea. It was the Passover holiday, and families were gathered for swimming, picnicking, fishing, and boating. A couple of fishermen were casting their nets in the distance away from the holiday crowd. This is where Jesus recruited his disciples among the fishermen, performed the miracle of walking on water, and fed the multitude with five loaves of bread and two fishes. I watched the sun set and the moon rise from the shore. We stopped at Capernaum, the old town of Jesus where he preached in the synagogue and performed miracles. I viewed the excavation of St. Peter's mother-in-law's dwelling and paid respects in the modern church built over St. Peter's house. In Nazareth we visited the Basilica of the Annunciation, a contemporary church built over a Byzantine and Crusader church and the grotto where the angel Gabriel announced to Mary that she'd give birth to Jesus. The interior of the church is decorated with mosaics of the annunciation donated by various countries. I located the US, Mexico and Japan inside the church and outside the church, in the patio, I located the Philippines. This place, along with the other holy sites, was engaged in earnest preparation for the Pope's visit in May

I realize after this trip that I know little of these countries, and that my feeling of "otherness" stem from my ignorance of their history, culture, language, religion, and people. I knew them from romanticized accounts of ancient history and modern travel brochures. The Arabs, Muslims, Jews, Egyptians and various Christian sects who people these lands are strange to me and I do not understand their wars and religious beliefs and traditions.

They have a completely different alphabet, language, and calendar. These are truly foreign lands and foreign people, but the conversations I had with hotel porters, taxi drivers, tour guides, and a couple of friends held a familiar theme. They boiled down to the importance of family bonds, of a good job, of security from harm, a bright future for the children, and a belief in a divine power that will ensure a state of blissfulness after one confronts mortality. The stranger becomes oneself in the end. The traveler is the foreigner.

CHAPTER 10: Kibbutz

I've had Jewish professional colleagues who talked about volunteering in a kibbutz for a summer or for a year in the 70's, before launching their careers. They extolled it as a transformative experience of personal enrichment and a way to connect with their roots. I happened to schedule my Israeli trip on Passover, so I was very excited when my friend invited me to have Seder with her at her kibbutz, Kissufim. It is 1.5 kilometers from the Gaza strip, south of Tel Aviv, northwest of the Negev desert. The proximity to Gaza raised anxious concerns among my family and friends, but my friend's father still lived there (she lived in Tel Aviv) and she was going so I figured I'd be just as safe there as anywhere else. There were signs of the danger though, in the ongoing construction of bomb shelters in each residence. I rented a car and drove the 116 kilometers on sleek highways. I had no trouble as the driving was on the right as in the US and I had a GPS I named Golda. I was intrigued to learn more about the kibbutzim movement when my friend remarked that people in Israel could tell when they met her that she was raised in a kibbutz. I couldn't, but surely the telling characteristics were positive.

The kibbutz movement focuses on communal living and socialist principles of joint ownership and community. Together with the Zionist movement it was a powerful force in establishing the state of Israel.

The first kibbutz was founded in 1909 by Russian youths in the southern shores of Galilee, in Degania. Kissufim was founded in the 50's by immigrants from South America and the US. My friend's father was one of the founders.

Early life in the kibbutz was harsh. Palestine, after the demise of the Ottoman Empire was barren and ridden with malaria. The resident Arabs were poor and lived in miserable conditions. The Jewish settlers drained marshes, irrigated the desert, planted the land and developed a thriving agriculture economy. Later, they expanded into manufacturing, services, electronics and other industry. With the creation of the state of Israel in 1948, kibbutzim grew rapidly until it declined in the 80's due to various factors such as economic recession worldwide, decline of agriculture revenues, and ideological shifts towards individualism. Today there are about two hundred and sixty kibbutzim ranging in size from less than one hundred members to over a thousand. The ideology is changing towards privatization, and there are some who profess its demise. Others, though, maintain optimism that it can adapt to economic realities while retaining its core principle of egalitarianism. Today many kibbutzim are moving towards eco-agriculture and tourism to maintain their vitality.

Kissufim now has dwindled to about one hundred members, and many are aging. Its economy is fueled by agriculture and dairy production, and it employs outside labor (Arabs and Vietnamese) to provide its workforce. The dining room is no longer the hub of the commune. My friend's father has a caregiver and eats at home, but his needs are taken care of by the commune. Some are moving back with young children by choice. The kibbutzim no longer raise children in separate quarters from their parents since the 70's, like how my friend was raised, so families find the commune ideal to shield children from the onslaught of external influences. And some young couples move back to escape the stress of urban living. Maybe, it is not a lost world

CHAPTER 11: Hiroshima and Nagasaki

To while away the two and a half hour drive to Hiroshima we folded origami cranes and learned the story of Sadako and the Thousand Paper Cranes. She was two years old when the bomb was dropped and twelve years old when she died of leukemia. Her mother referred to her illness as "atom-bomb disease". She was very brave and optimistic and her story is read by schoolchildren all over Japan and in many countries. She has become the symbol for hope for lasting peace in the world. The Children's Peace Monument in Hiroshima Peace Memorial Park, has a golden crane chime, and is dedicated to her and the thousands of children who were killed by the bomb. Thousands of paper cranes are offered to it daily by children from all over the world. In Nagasaki these thousand paper crane offerings are fashioned into art works by the children and dedicated to peace. They are heartbreaking to see.

As I ponder images of Hiroshima and Nagasaki after the A-bomb, a man-made destruction, I recall the dramatic TV images of the tsunami played over and over again in the news . These ruins are very similar. The monumental loss of lives and the rubble made of cities in the wake of the earthquake and tsunami of March 11 in Fukushima is a natural disaster. The devastation of Nagasaki and Hiroshima is not natural, it is the result of Man's will. Mankind should all visit the monuments in Hiroshima and Nagasaki and learn the story of Sadako and fold 1000 paper cranes for peace.

CHAPTER 12: Japan's "Otherness"

Japan impresses you as soon as you arrive. Kansai International Airport is a breathtaking space. It is a sparkling, man-made island with an efficient, ultra-modern terminal designed by Renzo Piano, and everywhere you look, high-tech amenities abound. In the rest room, for example, I study how to use heated toilet seats with buttons that control the temperature of your bidet and spray, and browse options for music or flushing sounds that muffle the revealing noise of bodily functions. Arrival and customs processing is easy to navigate with Kanji signs and English subtitles, and immigration staff guiding you and bowing profusely.

This bowing is universal, and seems to be a part of the natural gesture here. A hard hat worker at a road repair site bows deeply at the waist before giving me the crossing sign. A waitress bows before handing me a menu, serving my meal or saying good bye when I leave. Every greeting is accompanied by a bow and a smile. Our bus driver bows as we get in the bus, no matter how many times a day. Every interaction with another is preceded by a bow. This respect and politeness is a national characteristic. In the metro, I embarrass myself when I just hop on, not noticing beforehand that everyone automatically falls in line to board the train and waits for passengers to disembark first. Nobody turns away if you approach with a question, even if they can't speak English. If they can't decipher anything, they go out of their way to find someone who can help.

They are very tidy and clean here, obsessively so. In many restaurants there are baskets or decorated bins on the floor for your purse and things. In Japanese restaurants where there's tatami or polished floors, I take off my shoes, but slippers are provided and there are cubbyholes for my shoes. There are separate slippers for the toilet. In public toilets, there are big and small hooks to hang stuff, or wide ledges or compartments to accommodate shopping bags. There are sanitizer dispensers and a baby seat so you don't have to set the baby on the floor. There is no urine smell in the metro, and no graffiti. The toilets are spotless. The people here wear surgical masks to protect themselves from pollen and others from their cold. There are umbrella caddies, and if there is none, they will hand you a plastic sock for your wet umbrella..

The vending machines here blow me away. At rest stops on the road there is always a bank of vending machines to dispense everything from beer to toys. The coffee vending machine dispenses freshly ground and brewed coffee, and I can control the brew strength and fix it with cream or sugar, or even make it espresso or cappuccino. While it is preparing the coffee, there's a digital timer to tell me when it will be done and in the meantime the machine plays a rumba to entertain me while I wait. When the coffee is done, it tells me so and it opens the serving box automatically. Too much! I like the rumba though. If I don't have two minutes for individually brewed fresh ground coffee, there is canned pre-brewed coffee dispensed hot. It also dispenses a warning to be careful, because the coffee is hot. Even the machines are polite.

Japan is in the details. Meticulous, structured, everything in its place. The lunch boxes are wrapped in beautiful paper, and have many compartments to organize each food item, it looks like a gift box. Meal items are served in individual unique dishes that are themselves works of art. Outside, the cherry blossom is in abundance, present in ubiquitous floral arrangements in elegant ikebana style. Their arrangement seems simple, but their design is actually governed by principles derived from nature. This can be appreciated fully in the classic Japanese garden. The formal tea ceremony is indeed a ceremony with protocols and etiquette to be followed. Kabuki theater is enjoyed more if its traditions and art form are understood. It can be compared to opera, rich in showmanship, elaborately designed costumes, eye-catching make-up, outlandish wigs, and most importantly, exaggerated actions performed by the actors. The highly-stylized movements serve to convey meaning to the audience. It originated in the 17th century, during the Edo period, and originally performed by women for the common class, but evolved as entertainment for royalty, and nowadays performed exclusively by male actors portraying both male and female roles. It has been named as a UNESCO Intangible Cultural Heritage.

Japan is discipline. There are rules of conduct posted all over for the public, the underlying theme being consideration for the public good and to not interfere with another person's comfort. These signs are verbose and polite. Next to a coffee vending machine, "Please be careful, your coffee is very hot". In the Metro, "Please turn off your cell phones and do not talk on the phone, it may disturb the person next to you. On a balcony ledge, "Please do not engage in dangerous acts such as leaning over, as it might cause an accident." In the theater, "Please do not take photos during the show, the flash may distract the performer and disturb the show for others. This discipline and consideration for the common good is displayed so powerfully following the 3/11 tragedy. An observer remarked that the people acted in concert as if trained to behave that way, like an army. This seems to be a strong cultural characteristic of the Japanese, and has served the country well in a time of adversity.

Boarding the metro during rush hour I feel spooked surrounded by all these men in black, as if I am in a funeral caboose. Japan dresses formally. Men and women go to offices in dark suits, and children go to school in uniforms. Female broadcasters dress conservatively, with no cleavage showing. In rebellion to all this constriction of self-expression, a group of young people has developed a distinct subculture, the otaku. They dress in costumes and play roles. They have quite a following and reputation and they have become tourist attractions in the places they congregate, in the districts where manga, anime, and video games are sold, such as Akihebara, Takeshita dori, and Harajuku. Adult males with a large bank account can relax with geishas and kick off their shoes, and the ordinary salaried men can go to bars after work and hang out with other guys or visit Shinjuku's Kabukicho (red light) district or Ueno's Ameyoyokocho for adult role play. Alas, Japanese society is male-dominated, and as evidenced by the popularity of maid bars, the woman's role is to serve. Here, for a sum, a guy can hire a "maid" dressed in uniform of a short skirt, ruffled apron, high boots, and plenty of cleavage showing and can engage in master/servant fantasy. The maid will call him master, may groom him, even clean his ears, serve him tea, pamper him, etc. But even here, he can't escape from rules; in fact there are ten rules he has to observe. For example, he should not touch a maid's body, ask for a maid's personal contact information, or otherwise invade her personal privacy, that he not photograph maids or the café interior. Some of these maid's bars cater to women, and men become the servants and do the woman's bidding. Perhaps from this fringe culture societal attitudes are changing?

Japan has the romance of a long past. Medieval and feudal lore of the samurai and ninja, of royalty and chivalry, are oft repeated and beloved. Its art, culture and science go back over 2000 years and yet somehow Japan is still very young. It did not have a coming out until the Meiji restoration in the 19th century, the beginning of modern Japan. And while its feudal relics and structures are well preserved or faithfully restored, its cities have been reduced to rubble by modern wars, by earthquakes, the atom bomb, and, recently the tsunami. Because of this, entire cities have been rebuilt, and now sport the sleek and futuristic ambiance of modern architecture. Its infrastructure is similarly impressive. Overpasses and bridges and sky-ways interlock and loop over cities. Its rails carry trains with speeds like bullets, and its roads cut through mountains with tunnels instead of going around. Driving from Takayama to Lake Suwa, one of us counted twenty-nine tunnels, one of which was eleven kilometers long.

The Yoschino cherry blossoms are magnificent, and are the color of the lightest blush and transparent against the sun. When the wind blows and scatter the petals they float like snowflakes, breathtaking to behold. They're ephemeral, lasting only two weeks, but then the Kansai cherries take over, and the Iris, azaleas take their turn. And when fall arrives, the landscape is a brilliant red with the Japanese maples in full color and the Ginko trees turn yellow. These two times of the year it seems all of Japan is out to view their grandeur. There are numerous festivals throughout the year to celebrate nature's beauty and bounty. In the spring, there are hanami viewing parties under the cherry blossoms.

I enjoyed Japan, it is kirei (beautiful) and subarashii (magnificent), but it is too much of another world than my world.

CHAPTER 13: Myanmar

Yangon

In spite of having all my papers in order, I had a delay in processing my visa in Yangon. The officer spoke very little English. He refused to accept my cash to pay for the $30 fee, and I had to get my tour guide to interpret. The problem was that my money had a fold in it. It was a fresh bill without any blemish or tears at all, and still very crisp. I only folded it once to fit it into my wallet, but apparently he wanted a pristine one just off the press. I had him go through all my bills to select what was acceptable, and he reluctantly picked one, and stamped my visa. Later, when I tried to exchange for the local currency, the Myanmar Kyat, all my bills were refused because the serial number did not start with AB. Apparently it had something to do with counterfeit $100 bills. My tour guide told me not to worry, that he could get my dollars converted on the black market. I'd get a lower exchange rate, of course. I could not use my credit cards or my ATM debit card anywhere. The banking system we take for granted, with its easy loans, interbank operations, credit cards, bank cards, and so forth is nonexistent here. The country runs on a cash basis. The locals just shrug it off. There's the black market that deals with it, and life goes on. Why sweat the details?

Aung San Suu Kyi is beloved and popular. She is the political opposition leader who was under house arrest for twenty-one years and recently released. She was awarded the Nobel Peace Prize in 1991. People were holding their breath and preparing for the worst in anticipation of elections next month. News a few hours ago said she had fallen ill with vomiting, had to get IV drip, and that she had suspended her campaigning.

MOTORBIKES ARE BANNED IN YANGON! Not a single one of these ubiquitous and affordable transports, so popular throughout Southeast Asia, were on the streets. One myth about the ban is that a person on a motorbike made a threatening gesture to a military general. Another is that a motorbike rider distributed pro-democracy leaflets, and yet another is that a general's son was killed while riding a motorbike. The official line is that they are used by criminals for their activities, and that they pose a public safety hazard. Yangon downtown looked half in ruins between its old decaying buildings and deteriorating unfinished new structures. There are high rise luxury condominium developments that are uncompleted because investors halted financing the project. They gave up rather than put up with powers who kept on changing the rules. The military government, however, has built an opulent new capital city, moving the capital from Yangon to Naypyidaw in 2006. It is off limits to tourists and ordinary citizens. It is populated by government workers who can't afford to live there, and so according to my guide it is abandoned at night and becomes a ghost city. It is rumored that bomb shelters are underground, reserved for the military.

In Myanmar, Facebook and many websites are blocked, but the people find ways to go around that and in fact I was able to log into Facebook at The Strand Hotel. However, there are very few who own computers, internet cafes are sparse, and the country is not generally connected except at the major tourist cities. There are also frequent blackouts, and pfft! There goes your email before you could send it. New cars are unaffordable, costing about a hundred thousand dollars, and so many cars are gasping along that go way back into the 50's. Myanmar was never a Havana so they don't have those colorful vintage beauties on the road, just clunkers. The people still wear traditional dress for everyday. The men wear the sarong-like longyi. The women wear no modern make-up but the pasty cream thanaka. It is made from the ground bark of the namesake tree, yellow-ochre in color. It cools their skin, tightens the pores, and controls oiliness. They paint it on their faces in circles or like a mask, and on their arms, and it also serves as a sunscreen.

Many smiles here feature red teeth, stained and decayed from chewing kun-ya, red areca nut laced with lime and folded in a heart-shaped betel leaf. The practice is said to have been part of the culture for thousands of years, and it is common in Southeast Asia. My paternal grandparents chewed nga-nga, as it is known in the Philippines. As children we vied with each other to prepare the concoction for them. It is spicy hot, and produces a lot of saliva. Ptoo! You can hear the spit traveling in a precise trajectory, landing as a red stain on the pavement. I was careful to avoid stepping on a fresh one.

Street food is everywhere, and very cheap. My favorite was mont lin ma yar, a crispy snack with a rice flour pastry base that is topped with a quail egg, green onions and tomato.

The inconveniences of the city reflect the inefficiency and repressive policies of the government which had isolated the country for decades. The people here smile readily, are easy to approach, eager to help, children are happily playing, and the city has the bustle and vibe of energy. The antiquities are spectacular, magical, stunning, priceless. They're really treasures. The 2500-year-old Shwedagon Pagoda complex easily tops all the pagodas I'd visited. That is, until I'd gotten to Bagan.

Breathtaking Bagan

It is beyond words. Even pictures do not do it justice. It is more impressive than the Ginza pyramids, Angkor Vat, or Machu Picchu. It overwhelms with its vastness and the sheer number of stupas and pagodas that cover the plains and which run all the way to the Irrawaddy. Numbering ten thousand in the golden age between the eleventh to the thirteenth centuries, over two thousand survive today. From the humblest stupa to the opulent and gleaming golden Shwezigon Pagoda, each temple is a specimen of masterful craftsmanship. Even those that are in ruins retain a grandeur and elegance that still stand the test of time.

I visited at sunset. Climbing on top of a pagoda, I was overcome by the encompassing perspective of a high perch. Around me was a boundless display of beauty that seemed fit for a fairy tale. Just before the sun began to descend, the plain was visible up to the Irrawaddy and a cloudless blue sky stretched overhead. The temples are like conical mushrooms sprouting from the ground, in varying heights and sizes, with the patina of aged brick, red-brown and rose, peach and ochre. From my view above they are surrounded by green grass, small shrubs, and a sprinkling of red hibiscus and multicolored bougainvillea. There are few trees and they are crowned with graceful spreading branches that let light through like a lacy veil. My only company was my tour guide who was unobtrusive and allowed me solitude. As the sun began to touch the horizon the light softened, and the distant mountains on the other bank of the Irrawaddy began to dim. In a moment the sky was no longer blue, and the whole scene appeared washed in a hazy gray-green monochrome, obliterating the color of the stupas and outlining both they and the trees in shadow. When the sun hit the mountains and sat on the horizon, balancing like a big red cherry, the sky burst into color. Bands of yellow, pink, peach, violet and magenta blended like watercolor while the stupas, now in silhouette, fringed the feet of the mountains. The air was warm, but there was a light breeze, and the twitter of birds could be heard from the trees. A dog scurried beneath a shrub, and an ox cart ambled by. The hibiscus gave up its scent in the cooling night and wafted to where I sat, enthralled by the wonder of it all. Bagan is a center for Buddhist pilgrimage, and it is a spiritual place.

Inle Lake

I was met at the airport in HeHo by my Shan tour guide, an articulate young lady who is a member of one of the illustrious tribes in the Shan state. The Shan people are very proud of their long history and would like to restore their royalty to rule the region, which occupies about one-third of Myanmar's area. There is a strong movement for independence, and the military regime of Myanmar has difficulty suppressing armed resistance in the region. Myanmar had just opened up for tourism barely a year when I visited. For fifteen years it was closed to the world until sanctions began to be lifted in 2010. To experience this region in its unspoiled state, before tourism corrupts it, was a thrilling opportunity.

We took a motorboat to reach my accommodation, a resort hotel on the lake with individual cottages on stilts, built with local materials and techniques. The cottages are reached by meandering, connecting bridges and lit by candles at night. I have unobstructed views of the hills surrounding the lake and the expanse of the water. Inle is a highland fresh water lake, about 900 feet above sea level, and surrounded by mountains and villages of hill tribes. I arose at sunrise and saw the birds who call the lake their home circling above, noisily squawking and trilling as they dove to catch their breakfast. Through the morning mist I watched fishermen throw their nets into the water, their graceful silhouette framed against the light. Their boats are slender and shallow, carved from teak. On one end the fisherman stands on one leg and paddles with the other wrapped around the oar so that his hands are free. His net is inside a conical shaped frame made of bamboo. The frame has a wide base and tapering to the top, and is about twice as tall as a man. The lake is shallow in most parts, so the net with the open bottom is lowered to trap the fish, then the fisherman takes a spear to haul the fish up. It is most enchanting to see these boatmen paddling one legged on their boats as they go about their occupation, fishing or gathering seaweed or tending their floating gardens.

Once a year, at the end of September or early October, there is an 18-day festival during which the five Buddha images of Paung Daw U Pagoda are ceremonially rowed around the Lake in a colorful barge towed by the Inle leg rowers. Accompanied by pomp and reverence, the barge with the Buddhas will visit fourteen villages. There is a fierce race competition of leg rowers held in conjunction with the festival.

Life on the lake is much as it was a century ago, but it will not be for long.

The Road to Mandalay

Uninspired 70's buildings, bamboo and thatched huts, vendors crowding and littering the avenues, and food stands serving a mass of sweaty, unwashed patrons in the 104 degree heat. This scene killed all the romantic nostalgia I'd dreamed up reading and learning about this land. The Irrawaddy, that great river that springs from the Himalayas and cuts through the length of the country to empty into the Andaman Sea, is wrapped in noise from motorboats and will never know tranquility. Its banks are strewn with plastic bags and aluminum cans, and the dolphins that played in its waters will soon be just a memory.

The road to Mandalay is a swirl of dust and careening Toyota pick-up trucks converted to buses and groaning with heaps of passengers, produce, swine and fowl. Where the dawn burst out like thunder in the east, now it is a mellow red ball muted by the haze and smog of slash and burn agriculture and motorbike exhaust. But on Mandalay Hill you can still see the golden magnificence of the Mahamuni and the grandeur of the Kuthodaw. And a sweet Burmese lass, her cheeks painted with thanaka, still awaits her soldier to claim her and take her away to a land of milk and honey.

CHAPTER 14: Bhutan - The Last Shangri-La

March 2014

As my Drukair flight took off from one of the most dangerous airports in the world, Bhutan's Paro International Airport, I made sure I was seated for the best view of the Himalayas. The take-off was unexpectedly exciting. I leaned with all the pitches and turns that the plane took to avoid the mountains that hemmed the narrow, short, and deep runway. It barely avoided the sloping rooftops of the traditionally built houses with their intricately carved wooden eaves and rafters, small arched windows, and colorfully painted frontages of auspicious Buddhist symbols. It tilted severely left, then, as we seemed headed to strike the side of the mountain, it tilted right then left again like we were sashaying. It advanced towards a solid wall of pines and firs, and then suddenly lifted and cleared the top of the ridge into the clouds and open sky. The ice-peaked Himalayas glistened above the clouds, and flying over Kathmandu I saw the familiar silhouette of Mt. Everest. The vast Himalayan range provided the scenery until we crossed into India. Breathtaking!

I arrived in the capital Thimpu a day after the whole world celebrated the International Day of Happiness on March 20. The UN General Assembly established the event in 2012 after being inspired by Bhutan's philosophy of measuring the nation's development progress in terms of GNH, gross national happiness, instead of GDP, gross domestic product. I was intrigued to see for myself if this tiny Buddhist Himalayan kingdom, the Land of the Thunder Dragon, sandwiched between China and India, was for real. I became curious after accidentally coming across articles about the country during my 2011 research of Southeast Asia. Its crown prince, Jigme Wangchuck, charmed the whole county during his visit to Thailand in 2006 to celebrate King Bhumibol's 60th anniversary on the throne. The youngest among twenty-five royal guests, he was dubbed Prince Charming, and all the young women swooned and fantasized about meeting him. After the visit, travel to Bhutan from Thailand became very popular. He had the same effect when he went to Japan in 2011, in spite of being accompanied by his new bride. Tourism from Japan surged. From there on, each article I came across became more delicious than the last.

In 2007, he sold his BMW at auction to raise funds to start a radio station for youth, Kuzoo FM. He was educated in Massachusetts and England. He got married to a Bhutanese commoner in 2011 in an elaborate ceremony that went on for days. They were in love and lived together before tying the knot and he proclaimed, unlike his father who has four wives, all sisters, that he will only have this one wife. Polygamy is legal in Bhutan, as is polyandry, but it's becoming rare due to the expense of supporting each spouse equally. Women and men in many ways are equal in this society which began modernizing only in the mid-50's. Men and women work together in the fields, in road work, and even in construction. Both can receive education. In the 50's, during the construction of Bhutan's first road, foreign labor was prohibited. Each household was required to provide a worker, regardless of sex, to build the nation's highway. Nowadays labor is contracted from Nepal or India and governed by strictly enforced temporary work permits.

The story of Bhutan is the story of the Wangchuck dynasty, which consolidated power in the first king in 1907. The landlocked kingdom was isolated to the world until the reign of the third king in the 50's. He was educated abroad and started the change from a feudal society to a modern one. He got rid of serfdom and slavery, built roads, hospitals and schools. He died of a heart attack, and the fourth king took over at a tender age of seventeen. The fourth king moved towards democratization, introduced the philosophy of GNH to guide the country's development and promoted tourism. He allowed TV in 1999 and the internet and telephones. He did not want a repeat of his experience of suddenly having to rule without adequate training, and so, while still able to share his expertise, he abdicated in favor of his son in 2008, which stunned the nation. The fifth king, the Prince Charming, will preside over the transition from absolute monarchy to constitutional monarchy, and oversee the democratization transformation.

Bhutan is feeling growing pains, however, having only debuted into the modern world in the 50's. It seems to sincerely want to accomplish its lofty goals of democratization, of balancing development and the well-being of its citizens, of preserving its culture while pursuing modernization, and of preserving its environment while harnessing its natural resources. The ruling body has transmitted these ideals into a slick marketing of the Bhutan brand and the philosophy of GNH, but it had adopted contradictory autocratic and repressive methods. To preserve its culture, it purged the ethnic minority of Bhutanese residents of Nepalese origin, who had been in the country since its founding, and which constituted ten percent of its 700,000 population. Initially granted naturalized citizenship in the first Nationality Act of 1958, the law was amended in 1985 and disqualified their status. Subsequently they were stripped of their property, positions in government, and expelled as illegal immigrants. It mandated that the national dress, the Kira for women, and Gho for men should be worn in public place. It also mandated that citizens cannot criticize the monarchy, and though theoretically there is freedom of religion and separation of religion and state, Buddhism is the state religion, and the monastery and government assembly are housed in the same building complex in every state.

Buddhism informs the daily life of the people. The monks are consulted in every significant decision, and the religious hold a strong sway in how people think, act, or vote. The fourth king has four sisters for his wives because the monks prophesied that it would be auspicious. The coronation of the fifth king was on a specific date that was also auspicious, and so on with elections, travel, marriage, purchases, etc. There is so much superstition and magic and contradiction in the practice of religion. It frowns on killing but many eat meat, except they relegate the slaughtering of animals to Indian and Nepalese butchers. The simplicity and beauty and mysticism that the Buddha preached are lost in the hoi polloi.

The remote villages are still difficult to access. There is one East-West artery and radiating roads are skimpy. Travel even on short distances can take a long time because of the torturous mountain terrain, and it is often interrupted by landslides. Surplus produce from the farms cannot be transported to market except by walking several hours to reach the road. The government has built road-side covered sheds above these valleys so farmers can sell their goods to motorist. There is universal if inadequate health care, free education until the tenth grade, and competitive scholarships can be won for advanced study abroad. During the reign of the fourth king, the last absolute monarch, he distributed land. No one is homeless in Bhutan. Every farmer has a home in the traditional chalet style architecture with sloping hand pressed mud walls, intricately carved wood trims, and painted frontage. The villagers erect these homes for each other in a cooperative venture.

No one goes hungry in Bhutan. The farmers are self-sufficient, and the rare homeless or hungry, exclusively found in the cities, will find their way to the monasteries. There's hardly any crime or drug use. Marijuana grows wild, but it is used to feed pigs to increase their weight. Selling tobacco products is illegal and smoking in public is banned. In the cities the widening gap in income and culture is visible. The young generation change into T-shirts and jeans after school or work, and hang out in bars and shops, and watch English, American and Indian TV. They listen to foreign hit songs, surf the internet and use social media. Mobile phones are status symbols. They know about Sex and the City, wear brand apparel, are learning English, and dream of one day going to America or England to live the life they see on TV and pirated blockbuster movies.

Tourism is tightly controlled, and the number of visitors is restricted by a $250/day tariff and by limited seats on Drukair. Every tourist must be accompanied by a tour guide and be booked by a tour company, and tourist movement is checked at strategic posts. It is, however, worth it. The antiquities are impressive, the legends of the lamas spell-binding, and the mountain scenery is majestic. In early spring the deciduous magnolias and mountain rhododendrons are thick with bloom. Trekking is challenging and perhaps could provide spiritual contemplation, while the terraced hills and farmhouses give a peaceful, settled vibe. The air is fresh and the streets are swept clean. Food is organic and trendy, locally sourced from farm to table, and ema datshi, a chili-cheese dish, which had accompanied my meals throughout my stay, had become a favorite. The women are beautiful in their elegant Kira, a full length wrap-around held with jeweled pin at the shoulder and topped by a silk jacket. The gentlemen wear a Gho, a knee-length woven kimono or bathrobe-like wrap worn with knee high black socks and dress shoes. There are no touts, and hotel, restaurant, and tour staff are still shy about accepting tips. In another generation there will be no more Shangri-La, but hopefully there will be a young and vibrant nation which truly can balance the traditional with modernization and fulfill the promise of GNH.

CHAPTER 15: Galapagos

The wind is against the sail, and like a roller coaster plunging from its summit, the sudden speed registers in the belly with propulsive force that is scary and exhilarating at the same time. We are in top form, island hopping in the Galapagos in our wooden- hulled boat, built by Dutch artisans over a century ago. It has had a long career, adventuring first in the Baltics and the Northern Sea before retiring in the warm equatorial waters of Ecuador. The Sulidae is a twelve-passenger sailboat crewed by four laid back Ecuadorian sailors who fish for mackerel and grouper in the morning and grill them for supper. Served with pineapple, tomatoes and greens over rice and beans and flushed with fresh vino blanco from the Andes, they sustain our bodies for the exciting adventures ahead. With only seven guests on board, including the naturalist and tour guide, the three of us, my sister, her friend, and I, have a monopoly of the ship.

This is a good thing, because my luggage did not deplane with me from Atlanta to Quito. Delta said it would arrive on the next flight and that it would be forwarded to my next destination, in Puerto Ayora, where we were embarking. But it didn't arrive and already we are in the open sea and I don't have a stitch of garment to change with. The captain radios a large cruise ship in the vicinity so I can go shopping. Our little ancient sailboat glides alongside the multi-storied modern cruise liner and I climb the ladder to its spacious and gleaming lobby. Still hoping that I will be reunited with my luggage, I only bought basic toiletries, a bathing suit, a couple of panties and a pair of shorts and a T-shirt. My luggage never turned up until the end of the trip, to be collected in Atlanta. It went to Bogota and flew back minus the brand new leather backpack that I brought along for the hikes. Fortunately, I didn't need anything more than what I had cobbled together after all. I lived in my bathing suit, and slept in the T-shirt while the swim wear dried in the breeze.

The polished deck is our exclusive domain to sunbathe or read or gaze at the ship cutting the water and running with the wind. It feels like sailing in our private yacht, with our personal crew to attend to our comfort and pleasure. There was one glitch: we forgot to pack our CD's, and not having our music was the only misstep in this enthralling adventure. For eight nights and nine days, we overdosed on Jimmy Buffet and Cheeseburger in Paradise, the only American song carried by the crew among their old Spanish stand-bys.

At the time, in 1991, the Galapagos was known to me only through Darwin's work on the Origin of Species. It is a universe that is indeed very unique, and the lack of tourist infrastructure added an explorer's dimension to cruising. We pile in a dinghy to get on land. Many of the five hundred islands of this remote archipelago are desolate and barren volcanic protrusions from the ocean floor. We pick careful steps away from mummified, jagged lava, and step onto rope-like reliefs of the volcanic floor. Some of the islands here are of recent vintage from the latest fiery upheavals, and only the lava cactus and a few lichens survive in these arid and impoverished environments. From stark moonscapes to lush tropical forests and surrounded by a living ocean, Galapagos supports a diverse ecosystem that is a world unto itself. It is Spring, life in its elemental form is on display. Blue footed boobies in various stages of reproduction littered the geologically older islands. They are fearless as we slowly approach, and we come so close that we could see the heave and ebb of their chests.

Male frigate birds primp and strut by blowing their brilliant red throat pouches into swollen balloons to seduce a mate. Pre-historic looking marine iguanas duck in and out of lava rocks, looking for the perfect perch on which to catch the sun. You can take a close-up photo of their barnacles and they just stay still and stare, and you can see the vitreous humor in their eyes. The giant sea tortoise is so gentle it lets you pet it. Galapagos penguins, the only species of penguin found north of the equator, waddle to the ocean to cool off from the equatorial sun in midday. In the highlands we identify some of Darwin's finches, and we are excited. We visit red and black beaches washed with sands extruded from various volcanic eruptions, and pristine white beaches formed by coral reefs. We lay next to playful sea lions and fur seals on these beaches and in the water they swim with us and synchronize their movements within inches beside us, teasing but never touching. Incredible!

At night, with the sails full and the boat sleek and swift on the water, the whole ocean around us and the stars and constellations bright and twinkling above, it's like we're in heaven. We can see the moon and Venus, and the Southern Cross. There's phosphorescence in the water, shimmering on dolphins swimming alongside, the moonlight bouncing on their backs. Is this paradise?

CHAPTER 16: Alaska

We disembarked our Alaska Inner Passage cruise in Vancouver, so while there my sister Bonnie and I decided to explore Victoria. We'd heard so much about the Empress Hotel, so we booked an overnight stay. While reviewing our return flight details to Atlanta in the opulent and uppity tea room of the hotel, we discovered that the earliest ferry to Vancouver would not leave until our flight would be well on the way to Atlanta. We had to give up our reservation so we could return to Vancouver on the last ferry, and make our early flight. There was a long line of tourists hoping to get a room at the hotel, so the room we gave up had a happy taker. We didn't suspect that anything was unusual about the long line for a room. We assumed the Empress was always a popular choice, until we tried to get a hotel in Vancouver. We were informed it was British Columbia Day and there was no room available within 100 miles of the city. We ended up spending the night playing cards at the lobby of the airport Marriott, trying to stay awake with coffee all night.

That was one of the misadventures that made our Alaska Inner Passage cruise memorable.

In Sitka, we were gung-ho on a sea kayaking expedition that explored the native wildlife and vegetation from the magnificent waters of the Alaskan Gulf. It looked too easy to paddle this flimsy two-man fiberglass vessel, so my sister and I declined to separate for a rower, flexed our muscles to show that we weren't weaklings, and pushed off excitedly with hopes to spot bears, bald eagles and whales. Well, we overestimated ourselves. We huffed and puffed, but the current worked against us and we couldn't advance our watercraft. We lagged hopelessly behind the group and when the guide came back for us, we shamefacedly agreed to be hitched to him to be towed.

In Juneau I was excited to discover that there was a golf course and promptly made tee time joining a foursome of golf fanatics like me. I thought that it was a thrill to play golf in Alaska, never mind that it was only a nine-hole course and that we were issued mismatched and rusty golf clubs, and that the fairways and greens were in a sorry state of neglect. But the view was unbeatable, with glaciers and white mountains around and firs exhaling a crisp fragrance which seemed with each breath to clear up the city smog in my lungs. The course was criss-crossed by small shallow streams of rushing crystal clear water littered with thigh sized fat salmon, all dead and clogging the stream. I was horrified. I couldn't believe that this place was so polluted that it could kill all of the salmon. Then it hit me, that these were the salmon that died after spawning, a natural phenomenon. I still couldn't believe it, that they really died in such huge numbers, that their life cycle was indeed like that. But such is life, and death is a renewal.

Later, as we explored Juneau, we discovered many Filipinos who owned souvenir shops, crafts stores, and businesses downtown and we found two Filipino restaurants and a big Filipino-American Center. Filipinos are the largest Asian minority in Alaska and had been known to settle there since 1778. They were sailors and fur traders, known as Manila men. In the early 20th century, when the Philippines was a US protectorate after it was acquired from Spain at the end of the Spanish-American War in 1898, huge numbers were recruited to work in the salmon canneries in the winter, migrants from the agricultural fields in California. When the Immigration and Nationality laws were changed in 1965, it paved the way for family reunification, and abolished the national origins quota. Filipinos already in the US could petition relatives according to relationship preference criteria. The Filipinos we met were many generations removed from the original Manila men, and were thoroughly Americanized in their accents and lifestyles, but still deeply connected to their heritage. This was another unbelievable revelation to me, a lesson in history that was compelling and deeply moving. Alaska, that remote whiteness at the top of the continent, became very familiar, like family.

CHAPTER 17: Pacific Mysteries, Country Club Cruising with Oceania

April 18-May 6, 2013

Marlon Brando and his movie, "Mutiny on the Bounty", and Paul Gauguin's paintings of an island paradise populated by languid and sensuous women fire the imagination with exotic fantasies and build a desire to see for oneself what this is all about. When a friend I'd met from a tour of Cuba last year expressed an interest to share a stateroom for a cruise anywhere of my choosing I quickly jumped on the opportunity and unbelievably found this cruise with all the destinations I wished to visit. I'd just returned from a trip to Brazil, but if I didn't book immediately, I would have to wait until next year, because this was the ship's last South Pacific cruise before being repositioned to the Caribbean. There was no question of postponing it. I've been looking into this South Pacific destinations, especially to Tahiti, Papeete, Bora-Bora, Pitcairn, and Easter island for some time, and traveling there would require coordinating land, water, and air transportation, not to mention accommodations. It didn't require much deliberation to realize that this cruise was very affordable.

We flew to Papeete to board our ship, a two-year old medium sized luxury 5.5 stars cruise ship with about 1000 passengers and 800 crew, the latter an international mix of Italians, Indians, Czechs, Polish, Ukrainians, Croatians, Filipinos, Malaysian, US Americans, South Americans, British, French, Greeks, etc. My excitement quickly nosedived however, when I saw that my fellow passengers were 99.9% geriatric. OMG! They were not only very old, but many were disabled, moving with canes, walkers, or rolling wheelchairs. Those who moved unaided walked with the slow, shuffling, wide-based and flat-footed gait of Parkinson's, and men and women everywhere have the bent postures that signal osteoporosis. There are easily recognized signs of chronic cardiac failure in many with chronic pedal edema and leathered elephant legs. When you get in a crowded elevator, there is the peculiar scent of the aged, reminding me of consultations I did in nursing homes.

In Bora Bora a couple got off ship for medical treatment after the wife had a fall in the library, and then flew to rejoin the cruise in Fakarava. The tour director, while not very old but had medical issues also got off in Bora Bora together with her spouse who was also one of the entertainers, never to rejoin the ship. This required reshuffling of the ship's staff, resulting in the assistant tour director being promoted and doubling as the alternate entertainer also. In Huahine a man on coumadin misstepped while climbing the tour bus and cut his legs on the running board, which required fourteen stitches and looked more ominous by copious bleeding. He is diabetic and has peripheral neuropathy. The ultimate catastrophe occurred after Fakarava. A woman fell which broke her femur which caused the cancellation of the next port of call in Pitcairn Island, forcing us to be at sea for four days to get to Rapa Nui (Easter Island) where she could get medical attention. This left everyone disgruntled, and I was particularly unsympathetic, saying carelessly without examining the patient that it wasn't life threatening and if she can wait three days, another day would not make a difference, and we could then drop anchor on Pitcairn Island. A fracture, if not displaced and without bleeding, can be stabilized by splints. Later I learned that she had other complicating medical issues, and of course after my initial indiscretion, I acknowledged I was wrong and irresponsible. This cruise which started in Papeete, would call on the French Polynesian Islands and included the British Pitcairn Island and Easter Island in Chile and terminate in Lima, Peru. I booked this cruise especially for Pitcairn, of Mutiny on the Bounty's fame, as not too many ships stop there, so there goes my fantasy, still un-lived.

But all these led me to contemplate the issue of aging and my reaction to it. I have faced my fear. It is not death, for I do not believe in an afterlife and in judgment day. To me death is just the end of life, and my only wish is for it to be quick, and without suffering. Death is more a problem for the living that have to bury you, settle your estate taxes, and sort out your material possessions. I do not wish to impose this on my loved ones so I have simplified my affairs. I have divested myself of unnecessary objects, left instructions for my remains, and I'm spending my children's inheritance so they won't have to worry about estate taxes. My fear is aging into feebleness and dependency. Acknowledging this allowed me to see my geriatric fellow travelers in a different light. Cruise travel is like being cocooned. Everything is planned and organized for you, all your needs are attended to. You are reminded of important things to do, the service people fulfill your reasonable requests with a smile, your bed is made, your meals cooked, you are entertained, and within all this structure there is room for personal pursuits and enrichment if one wishes. In cruises, feeble and disabled seniors are enabled to engage in new experiences in a sheltered environment, they travel the world and socialize, and continue to accrue memories and fresh stories to tell.

Enlightenment achieved, I can now enjoy my fellow passengers and revel in the luxurious appointments of Oceania's Marina and look forward to our ports of call. I found a small group of late nighters who hung out in Horizons, the dancing venue presided over by Siglo, a talented Filipino band. Days at sea are crowded with a medley of activities but you can find me at my morning workout in the Spa and on the three-mile walk of the sports deck. Later, I'm painting with Artist in Residence Graham Denison, playing the Trivia Challenge with my team, "Seize the Day" and trying my hand at the Obstacle Putting Contest and in Jackpot Bingo, where I won the minor games three times for a total of $334 in prize money. I wasn't too lucky in the casino slots and I lost in the finals of the Blackjack tournament.

My roommate and I would go our separate ways during the day and come together in the evening for cocktails and music with Constantine at the piano or with the Orpheus String Quartet. Afterwards, we'd eat dinner in the many fine specialty restaurants on board. Then it was off to the evening postprandial show or dancing or the casino. There was very little time left for reading or for just laying out in the sun poolside. This was just as well since I couldn't check emails and Facebook anyway. Internet is available, but the cost for connection is prohibitive. It is delivered not by high speed fiber optics but by a system of geo-synchronized satellite signals. It is painfully slow, and often down. I opted instead to spend on Martinis and wine, which were not included in the cruise price. When I needed solitude to recharge, I enjoyed sitting in our stateroom veranda at sunset, in awe of the vast Pacific Ocean, listening to soaring music from my iPhone and musing on the lives of the ancient Polynesians and what life would be like for their descendants if the Europeans never found them.

Polynesia is very much like the southern islands of the Philippines, though its terrain, flora, and fauna is not as complex and diverse. Development and tourism is changing the idea of paradise. In Bora Bora where the obscenely expensive resorts of St Regis and Four Seasons are built on sandbars across the lagoon, where their overwater bungalows go for upwards of $1000 a night, paradise living is designed as an escapist fantasy of catered services and fine dining done with island views. They were built to cater to millionaires, but ordinary salaried men can book a bungalow and live like one for a day. In the mainland, some resorts are left abandoned after the last hurricane, and some unfinished projects lay in ruins to the elements when funds ran out after the world financial collapse. Half of the 267,000 population resides in Tahiti, the capital, and its traffic will rival that of Atlanta any day. Huahini, still part of the Society Islands group, is still fairly unassuming and offers a contrast to overdeveloped Moorea, Bora Bora and Tahiti. In Fakarava, one of the more remote atolls of the Tuamotu group, it's possible to enjoy an unspoiled island getaway. Small, isolated beaches surround its perimeter, and as the archipelago was formed from the coral reefs, diving there is said to be spectacular. Its pristine ecosystem has been designated a UNESCO Biosphere Reserve. There is only one hotel on the island, White Sand Beach Resort.

In the past, between 1966 and 1996, two of the atolls in the Tuamotu had been used as nuclear test sites by the French government. Amid protests, over 181 bomb devices were exploded, and during this period the military provided significant local employment which of course disappeared after the testing was banned. Today unemployment is close to 12% and 25% of Polynesians live in poverty. Papeete is ringed with slums, almost exclusively occupied by indigenous Polynesians. On top of the heap, accounting for 80% of the region's income, are the French. In the middle are mixed races and the Chinese, the tradesmen class together with minor government employees, and in the lower rungs is the indigenous population.

On Saturday in Bora Bora our tour guide noted that Election Day was coming up, and that on the ballot was the choice between independence and the status quo. Our guide is for independence. He envisions a return to community living and living off the land and the fruits of the sea, a simple life. It may be too naive. French Polynesia is heavily subsidized by France, and it's possible France is losing money on it. Another local guide, however, seems to be doing very well for himself in the current system. After his government employment was terminated he bought a small sandbar island where he constructed a thatched hut, and with a boat he employs himself by providing lagoon tours and snorkeling. He took us to his little island, guarded by his two friendly mixed pit bull dogs. He has an electric generator so he can power his satellite TV. He receives cell phone signals, and there are plenty of clams, oysters, and fish in the reef. He has a small vegetable garden in the sand. When he feels like it, he takes his boat to the deep sea without tourists and delights in catching a big tuna or snapper and invites his family for a feast. He is friendly with his rich French neighbor who owns the bigger and coconut-blanketed island next to his, with its several guest cottages and large main house. He likes to join the guide on his fishing trips, and invites him to take down any number of coconuts anytime for his use. After the last storm not too long ago the guide's hut was inundated by the surf and floated away, but he built another one in a day. He seemed quite content and happy, taking life one day at a time.

CHAPTER 18: Oaxaca

I have not met another Filipino on this trip, and I've tried to find them. I've asked my expat contacts, their cleaning lady, storekeepers, taxi drivers, random people I happen to chat with, and waiters. They've known Filipinos in other places, but not here In Oaxaca. Filipino overseas workers (OFW) are important contributors to the Philippine economy, accounting for 13.5% of the country's GDP. I've met them in all of the countries I've visited, even in places as remote as Antarctica and in Easter Island. In Dubai, where I've been most recently, they are so ubiquitous that I thought for a moment that I was in the Philippines. Why are they not in Oaxaca? This piqued my curiosity about Filipino immigration to Mexico and prompted a scholarly search through Wikipedia. I found no direct link to my question, and overall, there was a dearth of information about modern immigration. It can't be because of the economy and security. There are Filipino enclaves in Pakistan, even Iraq, and Syria. Is it because of proximity to the US and that is the preferred destination? I suppose with all the problems of Mexican illegal immigration to the US, it would be foolish for Filipinos to enter from Mexico. Canada would be the obvious choice.

I got excited, though, when I found a blog by a Filipino tourist about a chance meeting with a clan in Oaxaca who descended from a Filipino who settled in the area during colonial times. Their great, great, grandfather, Lorenzo Paulo, was a fugitive sailor who jumped ship off the isthmus of Tehuantepec in Southern Mexico. He met their great, great-grandmother in Tijuana, near the U.S. border. As the trans-Pacific railway was being built, Paulo sought and found employment there. He and his wife moved south and finally settled in the coastal town of Salina Cruz, in the state of Oaxaca. In 1859, Benito Juarez, Mexico's first Indian president and the then governor of Oaxaca appointed

Lorenzo as chief of security of the port of Salina Cruz. He developed a reputation as a tough hombre and was referred to by his descendants as "patron Lorenzo."

I found another article about a researcher coming across a park named Parque Reyna Maganda in Espinalillo, near Acapulco. Maganda is a Tagalog word for beautiful. He discovered that the great grandmother of this large clan indeed came from the Philippines. I was excited to find these gems of information, but also wondered why there seems so little connection between the Philippines and Mexico in modern times. My father-in-law, whose father was a Spaniard from the continent, married a Filipina and had six children. Four remained in the Philippines, a sister returned to Spain, and a brother went to Mexico and started a family there with a Mexican wife. On my second visit to Oaxaca I made a point to drop by Mexico City and look up the Pellicers. I had a most warm welcome and happy encounter with the Mexico family branch. I'm delighted that they had not abandoned their Filipino heritage. Maru attends celebrations organized at the Philippine Embassy. But unless I'm not searching well, there's very little Filipino immigration to Mexico in modern times. Most of it happened during the colonial era, and again after the Spanish-American War when the Philippines became a US territory. Filipinos in Mexico have assimilated completely and are no longer an ethnic entity.

When Mexico started its fight for independence in 1810-1821, colonial governance of the Philippines was transferred to Spain. Prior to that, Spain administered its American, Caribbean and Pacific colonies through its Viceroy in New Spain, in Mexico. Filipinos stopped arriving in Mexico when the Manila-Acapulco Galleon trade was terminated in 1815. From 1565-1815 the Manila-Acapulco Galleons did not only carry porcelain, ivory, silk, and spices from Asia to Mexico but it also transported culture and language and flora and fauna and religious practices between the two ports. I was so amazed by the similarity of religious festivals, and to find similar fruits and plants, and familiar words. The mango was brought to Mexico, and mais (corn) was brought to the Philippines. I was in Oaxaca the week before Dia de los Muertos, and the preparations and graveyard festivities bring back childhood memories of similar practices in my mother's barrio. It was a big deal. We clean the grave site, plant flowers, bring food, and socialize with neighboring grave visitors. Children scare each other with ghost stories. The weekly markets here are called tianggui, and as in the Philippines, palenque, balimbim, calachuche, guayabano, nanay, tatay mean the same. When I joined a Tai Chi class at Parque Jardin Conzatti, the teacher introduced his namesake as tocayo. Our barong looks very similar to the Mexican shirt and many dances and songs are performed in the same way. I didn't know that "La Paloma" was a Mexican song, and not from Spain. It was a required piece in many piano teachers curriculum and one of the earlier challenges in my hard journey on the keyboard.

With 250 years of shared Spanish colonial history and culture between Mexico and the Philippines, I'm puzzled that there is no visible expression of this relationship in contemporary society. Both even have the common experience of being conquered by the U.S. In the Mexican-American War of 1846-1848, the U.S. annexed the whole American Southwest from Texas to California, and the Philippines became a US territory after the Spanish-American War in 1898 until July 4,1946. When I speak to the youth in both countries, and to those in the U.S., there is little familiarity with the common bonds that tied these three countries together in history. When once we were brothers, we have become strangers, and these days some may even harbor contempt for one another.

"One's destination is never a place, but a new way of seeing things." – Henry Miller

CHAPTER 19: Brazil

Carnaval

February 6-12, 2013

Carnaval is not what it seems. True, at its most obvious, it is the biggest party and parade in the world. The samba school competition and five-day parade in the week before lent beg for superlatives to describe them. One has to see it to believe the magnitude, the gigantic proportion, the over-the-top costumes and floats of the event. Each night, six samba schools are announced with fireworks, and each parade down the half mile 72,000 seats of the Sambodromo grandstand. Each samba school presents a behemoth spectacle organized around a theme, accompanied by specially composed samba music performed by a huge percussion and brass band, with a drum queen, selected after a fierce competition, who leads more than 3000 marchers in elaborate and themed costumes and about seven giant floats. The huge ensemble completes the half mile with a strict time schedule, and a night's show lasts until dawn, from 9pm-7am! We were comatose with sensory overload after the third school, and had to get back to the hotel dazed and dripping in sweat and beer.

Carnaval week brings around 900,000 foreign tourists to Rio, generating $628M for the city and $3.2B for the whole country. Each samba school, meanwhile, spends $3-4M each to put on their show. Financing these gigantic productions is a challenge for the samba schools, especially for the ones that are lesser-known, and drug and crime money have found their way into an endeavor funded by public grants and scholarships. The purists decry the commercialization and the high price of participation. The ordinary carioca will have a hard time coming up with the cost of a Sambodromo ticket, and to march in the parade requires buying the approved theme costume and paying for the privilege. So it appears the Sambodromo carnaval has left the people and gone corporate to serve the tourist industry. Still, there were five to six million people who came to Rio to party in one of the five-hundred blocos, street parades approved by the city, scheduled throughout the different neighborhoods, where anyone can participate for free. These consist of thousands of sweaty bodies in various states of undress or in outlandish costumes, with a can of beer in one hand, and dancing to samba music from a loudspeaker on a truck. We managed to parade with the multi-bloco group in Lapa. That Sunday 19,000 tourists went offshore from nine cruise ships and the temperature reached 102 degrees F. Need I say more?

Carnaval week is a holiday. Most stores along parade routes are boarded up for protection. Police are visible, and porta-Johns are erected in strategic locations. There is a fine for urinating in the street, but you can still smell urine everywhere, and the following day the accumulation of trash is too much for street sweepers to keep up with. In Cinelandia, only restaurants and souvenir shops are open. Banks are closed, and since most ATM's accepting foreign cards are in banks, we couldn't withdraw $R. We wanted to visit Petropolis, the Imperial summer capital, but it was closed.

In Copacabana we caught some of the street percussion bands, and the crowds were not as thick as they were in downtown Rio, and there's a nice boardwalk and beach to cool off on. We got the full flavor of the Carnaval by staying in the Copacabana Palace, where a standing room ticket to their ball cost $R1750, which we couldn't afford. Instead, we moved to downtown Rio and took the Metro from Cinelandia to the

Sambodromo on Sunday for $R6.40 RT. We were with hundreds of costumed passengers, and I still managed to get requests for pictures with my gigantic plumed orange Can-Can hat, purchased in a Lapa second hand shop. It was so huge that I couldn't pack it in my return luggage, so I left it in my hotel room.

We loved the visit to the hillside neighborhood of Santa Teresa with its colonial houses, cobbled street, boutique hotels, and fine restaurants. For many visitors, the main attraction is riding on the tram, which offers a spectacular hilltop view of Rio, the Sugarloaf mountain, and the Cristo Redentor on Corcovado. We weren't able to use it because it was undergoing repairs, and in the summer sun we hiked up to the top and found the vista ourselves. We discovered an upscale watering hole on the way down in the Hotel Santa Teresa, and then finished with a seafood lunch at Sobrenatural.

We had to squeeze into bikinis to be part of the Ipanema beach scene, and we learned the ritual of ordering a mate com limao and biscoito globo from an orange-uniformed beach vendor. We did the obligatory pilgrimage to Corcovado to pay our respects to Cristo Redentor and to marvel at the 360 degree panorama of Rio. From afar, without the close-up view of the favelas, Rio is very dramatic and picture perfect, with buildings marching down on its mountainside and spilling into the sea, surrounded by greenery and stone outcroppings and flanked by golden beaches and islands silhouetted against the horizon.

Ah, the favelas. We were advised not to say the word out loud, for it is disrespectful to the people living in the sprawling slums of Rio and the other urban centers of Brazil. The politically correct reference is the comunidad. The politically correct propaganda also states that Brazil is racially egalitarian, that Brazilians do not harbor racial prejudice towards one another, and that if social mobility is impeded, it is due to socio-economic class rather than racial factors. Nobody discusses race openly in

Brazil. Unlike the U.S., where it is acknowledged and banned institutionally, it is veiled and shamefaced in Brazil. Blacks comprise 51% of the population, but the overwhelming majority of people in the slums is Black. In the richer districts of Leblon and neighboring Ipanema, Blacks comprise only 7% of the population. White income is more than double that of Blacks. In universities only 6.3% is Black, and only1% of professors is Black.

Brazil was the biggest importer of slaves until its abolition in 1888, importing 4.9 million compared to the 400,000 imported to the US. After abolition, freed slaves were not hired in the work force and not offered citizenship. Instead, a policy of "whitening" was adopted. The government subsidized European immigration with free passage and employment. This was intended to replace the slave work force, and it was hoped that intermarriage would cancel out the black race. The experiment obviously failed, and was replaced by the racial democracy concept. It passed anti-discrimination legislation in the 1950's and its 1988 constitution made racism a crime. Enforcement, however, is rare. There is only one Black judge. In Dilma Roussef's cabinet there is only one Black member among thirty-eight. Air travel is dominated by White passengers, magazine covers feature White models, TV and film stars, business executives and professionals have White faces, and upscale shopping venues and restaurants have White clientele and Black service workers. The attitude, as it is in the U.S., is resistant to change. The ruling White class just assumes that Blacks belong to the bottom rung of the social ladder, and that the lighter the skin color becomes, the higher one's position becomes.

Slaves had regularly mounted rebellions during colonial times, and many escaped into the jungles and founded communities, the quilombos, which are only recently being recognized by the government and given access to services. It is a puzzle why there is only a rudimentary movement in raising consciousness and activism among Blacks.

The culture, music, and art being showcased in Brazil and which identifies Brazil is essentially developed from Black culture. It generates the multibillion dollar tourist industry, yet Blacks do not participate in its profits. This is starkly evident in Salvador. When the city decided to refurbish Pelourinho as a tourist destination, it evacuated the long-time and largely Black residents of the decaying city and resettled them in the periphery, where they could not participate in the city's renaissance. Pelourinho has virtually no local residents. It is populated by tourists, and its animation is created by business and restaurant owners and tourism officials who schedule events and programs to entertain tourists. It is Disneyland. Ironically, Pelourinho is named after the pillory that used to be in the town center, where slaves who transgressed were shackled and lashed publicly as a warning to others.

Having said that, the predominantly mixed race people I encountered as a tourist were very friendly and helpful, and indeed fun-loving and exuberant. I loved the food, and I developed a taste for acaraje, feijoada, coxinha, and moqueca, and of course the meat lover's churrascos. Muito bom. I got to know Carlinhos Brown, Ivete Sangalo, and more than samba. I got to listen to trio eletrico, axe, and discovered Bel Borba and Jorge Amado.

CHAPTER 20: Batanes

There is no question that the allure of Batanes lies in its remoteness, in the authenticity of its unspoiled landscape and people. There are the plunging cliffs and rugged, rocky coastlines set off by sandy coves and breaking surf. There are the infinite verdant pastures and rolling hills that frame grazing cattle and carabaos, and goats effortlessly climb steep slopes that seem to meet the clouds and blue sky. The morning mist casts a spell on the cracks of canyons and blankets the valleys, and the evening comes after the sun sets in the southern China Sea in kaleidoscopic splendor. On Tukon hill, where there is a chapel patterned after the architecture of vernacular houses, one can see the Pacific Ocean in the east and the South China Sea in the west. On a clear day you might just see Taiwan from the northernmost island of the ten-island Batanes group, a mere one-hundred kilometers away, nearer than its distance from mainland Luzon.

There are no big hotel chains, and hopefully, they will stay away forever. There are no Jollibees or Starbucks. Basco, the capital, only recently acquired twenty-four-hour electric service. The other two inhabited islands, Sabtan and Itbayat, get only sixteen and twelve hours of electricity. There are only hole-in-the-wall eating establishments, but the food is uniformly delicious and organic. The only pizza place, Napoli, delivers gourmet pizzas out of the owner's home. The inns accept walk-ins for meals and serve a du jour menu that depends on the daily catch and what was in the market. You can ask the inns to purchase certain foods from the market and cook it for you and they will oblige cheerfully. We liked the *pako* (fern) salad, the marinated dried *dibang* (flying fish), lobster, and the exotic and hard to catch *tatus* (coconut crab). There is internet in the town center, cell phone reception and TV, but no movie house. The B&B inns are pared down to basic amenities. The Honesty Cafe is an unattended convenience store and coffee shop where you pick what you like, list it, and then drop your payment in a slot. Breathtaking! The local garlic is reputed to have the most fragrant and sweet flavor, and the sweet potato and taro are plump and firm. The traditionally woven baskets are exquisite, but everything else is imported from the mainland and has Manila prices.

Sabtang, a forty-minute boat trip from Basco, is served by round-hulled boats different from the outrigger *bancas* of the rest of the Philippines. They are more like the early Viking boats, well-suited to ride the oftentimes choppy currents of the channel where the waters of the Pacific and China Sea collide, and the strong winds from Siberia blow. We didn't have time to visit Itbaya, where the ancient funeral caves of the Ivatans, the indigenous ancestors, were excavated. It is four hours away by these native boats or a fifteen-minute flight with a nine-seater plane, Skypasada, which also serves Tuguegarao. We met the ragtag crew of this airline at breakfast one morning who regaled us with their harrowing tales of flying through storms and fog, and nonchalantly dismissing these as part of a days' work.

Sabtang holds the largest number of occupied vernacular houses in the province, and is nominated to be included in the UNESCO Heritage Sites. It is a must see for its uniqueness. These houses are made of limestone and coral with a thatched *cogon* roof, and have a distinct architecture, a fusion of the early ethnic houses and European technology introduced by the Spaniards. The houses have withstood both the island's regular typhoons and the grueling test of time.

We embarked from the port of San Vicente, rising very early, and didn't realize we would be using the public boat and not a chartered tourist boat. We were with the locals and crowded by sacks of produce, motorcycles, hogs, chickens and other cargo. We were told that there was a shipment of Ginebra San Miguel (gin) which hadn't yet arrive at the port, so we would have to wait for it because the boatman didn't want to lose his revenue. Norma, the ultimate problem-solver, negotiated to have our group reimburse the boatman for the cargo's passage so that we could leave as quickly as possible, never mind the consequences that would befall the island with delayed delivery of such a vital cargo. The sea was choppy on the return trip, and the boat crested and slammed against the bigger waves, hurling buckets of ocean at us and soaking us to the bone. While trying to steady myself from falling off my seat as the boat lurched, something sharp lacerated my ankle as I stepped on canvas and fishing nets on the floor. The bleeding was out of proportion to the size of the cut (from low dose ASA intake prolonging coagulation) and Mars almost got decapitated by the bamboo steering pole that slipped from its mooring. However, the whole experience was authentic, and an adventure. Anchors, away!

I visited new friends who were staying at the Batanes Resort to check out the accommodations (I recommend the Itbayat and Sabtang cottages for the ocean view) and to watch the sunset from their beach. It was dark when I walked back to where I was staying at Seaside Lodge. There are no taxis, very few cars, a couple of jeepneys for inter-town travel, and the odd motorcycle. A couple of lone scooter riders stopped to offer me a ride, but I politely declined. Our tour guide assures, however, that the offer is sincere and without malice and no remuneration but a smile and a "thank you" is expected.

The authenticity and sincerity of the people beguiles and disarms, and is a breath of fresh air. We city slickers had to focus on going with the flow and being laid back and not sweating the small details. Going into zazen, if you will. The masseuse was two hours late, saying with a smile that she'd overslept. We rescheduled for after dinner, and after being late ourselves, we didn't get our massages until we were just about ready for bed. Likewise, our lunch caterer in Uyugan did not have lunch ready because she'd forgotten to put us in her schedule. Not to worry, she summoned her husband from the farm to help and she had a delicious lunch on the table in an hour. She had been a *barangay* chief for three terms and now she was running for the town council. She is a multi-tasker, and we empathized completely. Later that day we wanted a manicure but couldn't get an appointment from the three manicurists in town because they're all servicing a wedding, which by custom is attended by everyone. The reception was a street party, so we asked to join and we were enthusiastically welcomed. The boom box was blaring *carinyosa* and they were dancing the traditional folk dance. We got in the mood and I danced with the groom, and then another guest who already had too much *palek*, the local sugar cane brew. He wasn't going to let me go, and I didn't want to offend, so I was about to dance again but Lida rescued me and took me away. We were delighted to participate in the custom of giving a gift of money to the bride and groom.

People here smile and greet you warmly on the street. I was poking around the vernacular houses, curious about an occupied interior and the man of the house introduced his family and invited me for coffee. The mayor stopped to say hello and chatted with us. He bewailed the challenges of completing the UNESCO application process to designate Sabtang as a heritage site. He needed private funding and government support for restoration and maintenance which his small island could not undertake alone.

The countryside around evoked a nostalgic and bucolic scene. I saw a man knee-deep in the receding tide casting his net, a young boy tethering his goat, a farmer in the fields. I saw a basket weaver at her craft and carabaos grazing on hills and variegated hibiscus adorning roadside fences. The surf broke on the shore and exploded against volcanic cliffs, and there was a taste of the sea in the air. Is this paradise?

CHAPTER 21: Venice

Nov 2004

Venice is a Renaissance theme park, like a Michelangelo Disneyland. It is just like in the pictures; everywhere you go it's a Kodak opportunity. Johnny and I planned to do Venice for our Thanksgiving trip, before he died in January. I decided I'd go anyway, even alone. I'd travel by foot and without an itinerary, hopping off the vaporettos whenever I saw something interesting. It wasn't crowded, and the weather was partly sunny and without flooding. Most tourists here are Europeans, arriving by bus from the mainland. There are plenty of couples, and having overlooked that Venice is such a romantic city, it is painful to watch a young couple on their honeymoon, touching and gazing at each other lovingly. But the attractions of the city are too powerful for sad thoughts and are effective distractions until I see, on my way to Murano, a gondola carrying a coffin covered with flowers. It throws me off balance to see it rock while the surrounding vaporettos roughed the waters. I isolate the view in my camera and frame the gondola. I photograph it gliding elegantly on the calm canal, shimmering in the light of the autumn sun with the flowers over the coffin creating a burst of color and freshness that celebrated the dead. I ask where it is going and quickly take the vaporetto to Isola di San Michele, the Island of the Dead.

The island on approach doesn't look like a cemetery. It is wrapped in bright terra-cotta walls and interior tall cypress reaching to the sky. An arched boat entrance with white trim and ironworks guards the gate. There is a Renaissance church at the entrance. It is a beautiful place, tranquil, a perfect place for repose and meditation. I haven't had a quiet moment alone for months, having been too busy and too distracted by tasks. I wander among the dead, reading their names and studying how old they were when they died and who survives them. Pretty soon they seem like people I have known. As every deceased has a photograph on the grave, I could imagine the way they lived, and I could feel their personality through their expressions, clothing, and the wealth suggested by their resting place. As I walk, I stumble upon famous graves: Ezra Pound in the Protestant section, Diaghilev and Igor Stravinsky with his wife Vera lying next to him in the Orthodox Section. I meander among the more opulent mausoleums with their frilly ironwork and gated interiors, and see their occupants photographed within.

Following footpaths, I come upon a lush setting with full shrubs and tall cypresses whose height conjures exalted feeling, as if I were in a cathedral. I pause to meditate in the fifteenth century Chiese di San Michele, a magnificent Renaissance church dedicated to the Archangel Michael, the guardian of the cemetery. I miss Johnny very much. It is very peaceful there. The drone of the vaporettos seems very far away. There is no one else in the church but me. The walls are silent. There is a lingering scent of incense in the air, and an autumn glow is sneaking through the open door, illuminating the dust particles that whirl and jerk in a St. Vitus dance.

St. Vitus dance, in medical parlance, is a chorea, a neurologic movement disorder associated with rheumatic fever, and thinking of it reminds me of Mama. It is strange how free association can take on unexpected turns. Mama took care of Papa after he had a series of strokes which disabled his body and his mind. He died on January 23, 1993 at age eighty-three, but Mama had been a widow even before Papa's physical death, in that she functioned alone, and her life was never the same as when Papa was full of vitality and was her support and helpmate. But Mama was full of spunk. For twenty-five years, Mama lived independently. She reinvented herself, found a new role, a new identity, and respect.

As I leave the island this thought fills me with purposeful energy. My life will never be the same without Johnny, but while it is different it will be just as wonderful, and I am looking forward to it.

I set out to have a great time in Venice.

I hung out at the fresh market where they sell sparkling fish under tall arches of baroque buildings. The cheeses and smoked meats piled high on counters look like they're to die for, not to mention the patisserie and the gelatos, hand-made fresh every day! I check out Lido just to see what's it's all about. Lido beach is littered with cabanas that look like Porta-johns. I can't imagine how bathers find space to stretch and sun themselves. I stumble upon the Jewish section, the oldest ghetto in the world, where the word ghetto was first used to designate their segregated community. Shakespeare's famous Jew is from Venice, right? The theme park motif continues with evening entertainment. I go to a Chamber concert of Mozart, Bach, and Vivaldi with musicians in period costumes at the Doge's Prisons, and I crossed the disappointing footbridge of the Bridge of Sighs to get there. I go to an Opera concert of arias from Rossini, Mozart and Donizetti with more costumes at the Scoula di S. Teodoro.

At the osterias I have spaghetti with squid and black ink sauce and grilled seafood, and of course I have tiramisu, which originated here. Shopping is fabulous and actually cheap since the stores are boutiques and sell one of a kind items made by the artisans who own the shops. Knits, leather, Murano glass jewelry and serious gold and precious stone works are all mouth-watering, but my shopping budget is blown on one item, a ten-piece Murano glass creche with 24-K gold highlights which I have to carry by hand all the way to the US. The wines are expensive, and as in the US, I still can't afford the Barolos, Brunelos, and Amarones. A half bottle of Valpolicella is what I have with dinners, about Eu16. I have conversations with diners at the next table. People are very friendly, and European tourists want to practice their English so they are very chatty. My hotel is very charming, a refurbished palace just steps away from a vaporetto stop, very convenient, and a ten-minute walk to San Marco square and to the Rialto bridge. The place has old-world service, which is a treat after all the rudeness of the airline people on my way over.

They say that it's the holidays that's hard to bear after the death of a spouse. It's true, but it is also healing to reflect on the loss and to embrace the joy of living. I understood that here in Venice.

CHAPTER 22: Tassajara

August 2005

It had been a while since I had greeted the morning and I had forgotten how exhilarating it could be. At 5:20 am, the hand bells at Tassajara woke me up. The tinny, tinkling sounds meandered between the cottages and summoned me from sleep. I booked a tatami room, a 10x12 cottage shared with Anicia. It was furnished sparsely with reed mats, two double futon mattresses on the floor, and covered with plush down comforters. They kept us warm and cozy, when the temperatures plunged from 103F degrees during the day to under 45F at night. The room had low shoji screen windows that were just above my head from the futon on the floor. I looked up and peeked through the bamboo grove, which was still in darkness, and saw the glimmer of light in the sky. It was just a hint of light, and gradually, as if someone was turning the dimmer switch in a room, it brightened and muted light filled the surroundings.

The sound of wood mallet striking wood plank cracked the stillness, and the monks were summoned to Zazen at 5:50 am. Different sounds interrupted my dozing, signaling various activities for the monks. There was the riff of a distant drum-roll followed by slow beats, then brass gongs and finally the tolling of the giant railroad bell at 6:30 that jolted me to attention. Dawn had arrived, and light bathed the whole camp even though the sun wouldn't rise for another hour. Sharp, yellow rays struck the side of the mountain and erupted with exuberance. It spilt over into the cottages in a powerful presence that told me, palpably, that it was time to rise.

It was not easy to get to Tassajara, which is in the middle of the Ventana wilderness in California. It is located on the Santa Lucia Mountain of the Los Padres range, a remote place

112

accessible only by a steep fourteen-mile dirt road which frequently narrowed to a single lane. The final five-mile descent of the twisting road was a brake-burning plunge that stirred up a thick smoke of swirling dry earth. The dust settled completely over our car and obscured the windshield. A four-wheel drive was necessary to negotiate this terrain, but our rental car, a Hyundai Sonata had only the drive shift and no low gears. I trusted Anicia, who was driving, with my life and I was in Zazen even before we started our retreat. It normally took one hour and fifteen minutes to drive this fourteen-mile road, but Anicia, oblivious of endangering our lives, zipped through it in fifty minutes. The Buddhist Center sits on a fault that feeds the Tassajara hot springs. In the late nineteenth century, it catered to the imaginative few who saw its potential as a resort and healing center. It was burned down in the early twentieth century, and was not rebuilt until the 1950's when interest in Buddhism began to pick up in the West. A friend of the late Zen master Shunryu Suzuki suggested that the old resort site would be a perfect place to open a Zen Center. Thus the first practicing Zen monastery outside of Asia was built. Only in recent years have guests been able to stay at the center, and only during the summer season. For the rest of the year, the center functions strictly as a monastery.

The retreat was intense. It started with thirty minutes of sitting in silence at 8 am. This was a small approximation of Zazen. Paul looked the part of a Buddhist monk. He was ascetic in build with high cheekbones, hollow cheeks and dark eye sockets framed by a clean-shaved skull. He sat on his pretzel-twisted legs, right foot over the left thigh and vice versa, spine erect, chin forward, looking ahead in a hypnotized gaze and breathing evenly, silently, immobile and unshifting for the whole thirty minutes. I supposed he was capable of emptying his mind, the objective of Zazen. Meanwhile, I was trying to be very still, but I couldn't manage. My muscles started to quiver after three minutes and I was forced to make an ever so slight move to shift my weight. I had just had two cups of coffee on an empty stomach at 7:30 am. My alimentary tract rattled with borborygmi so loud you could hear it across the room. And I couldn't empty my mind. I peeked sideways to see what the others were doing. I stole a look at Paul. My mind wandered. What should I do after the session at 1 pm? Should I go to the Narrows and read or should I bathe in the swimming hole? Should I hike the Overlook Trail tomorrow?

That day at dawn, I hiked the Ridge Trail. The mountain wildflowers were covered in mist. The scent of Mexican heather and mountain sage filled the air, and the Yucca stood tall and arrogant over the trodden grass. Birds emerged from the trees and twittered calls as they hunted their breakfast. I caught myself and I tried to concentrate on serious thoughts. But then, thinking at all was wrong. I should empty my mind. That was the way to practice mindfulness, to be receptive and discover my true nature and self. I should concentrate on breathing and let all thoughts go and be with the here and now, open and without preconceptions. I should be that wave that becomes defined and individual upon the shore, but also one with the ocean where as a wave I came from, and to which I would return. Whew!

After a grueling morning of these sessions I was looking forward to lunch, which was announced by the sonorous tolling of the big old railroad bell. The vegetarian meals were delicious and very filling. The breads were especially famous and at the end of our stay, they'd bake a bunch of different varieties which we could purchase as a donation to the Zendo. Lunch offered an option of self-prepared boxed meal from a delectable array of spreads, salads, cheeses, vegetarian pates of almonds and sun-dried tomatoes, pestos, and condiments. Fruits and fresh greens and baked goods, completed the smorgasbord. On our way up the mountain, Anicia and I had stopped for a half case of wine. This proved to be a divine complement to the boxed meal. We took our picnic to the Narrows, the trail along Tassajara Creek, where in its nooks and crannies, we discovered secluded swimming holes. Along its banks were giant flat boulders. We spread our beach towel and sunned nude. It felt so guileless, a belonging and oneness with nature.

This was the moment when the Buddha in all of us would say, "Life and death is the same thing, it is something, and it is nothing."

Life will never be the same without Johnny. It will be different, I will have a rebirth.

CHAPTER 23: Camino Santiago de Compostela

When I volunteered as an English speaker in a Pueblo Ingles immersion language program for Spaniards, an extension of my retirement celebration in Spain, I learned about the Camino Santiago de Compostela. It is an ancient walking pilgrimage that goes back to medieval times and is very popular in Spain and Europe. Gradually, it has been acquiring devotees in the US. There are several routes all across Spain, Portugal and France, all terminating in Galicia at the Cathedral of Santiago de Compostela. The French route, Camino Frances, runs from St. Jean Pied de Port in France through the Pyrenees, the Meseta, and the mountains of Galicia, and is the most popular and well equipped with accommodations and services. Many undertake the arduous eight hundred kilometer trek for religious reasons, a holy pilgrimage. I had become a lapsed Catholic, but I was looking for ways to incorporate spirituality in my life.

I was thinking of how to mark my seventieth birthday. That was when the idea hit me like a lightning flash. I got excited and inspired.

When WWII broke out Mama was pregnant with me. Papa was working in Kalinga, Mountain Province. News of the Japanese landing in Lingayen Gulf and their rapid march to the interior spread quickly. MacArthur had been ordered to Australia and American commanders were surrendering. Philippine soldiers continued the resistance, and the mountains of the Cordilleras were logical sites to set up guerrilla camps. Mama and Papa were in dangerous territory and with transportation disrupted, they walked nine hundred kilometers from Kalinga, Mountain Province in the north to the Bicol Peninsula, south of Luzon. Joining the family in Pasacao, their coastal village, they fled to the hills of Suminabang to await the war. So I became excited with the idea that I would walk the Camino to mark my seventieth birthday and to celebrate Mama's trek from the mountains to the sea. The juxtaposition of our images, me in the womb as Mama walked and myself on my seventieth birthday was a profound reminder that I owe my birth to the safe environment that my mother sought in the chaos of war. In the process, I hoped to find my way to a more spiritual life.

I spent three days in Paris before proceeding to St Jean Pied de Port, in the French Basque, where I registered on August 2 for my Camino passport. This would be stamped officially along the route to document my pilgrimage. I would present this credential in Santiago, to receive my Compostela, the Pilgrim's certificate.

After getting off the TGV in Bayonne, I transferred to the local train which was crowded with *peregrinos* all revved up and spontaneous in camaraderie. There were many languages spoken, but somehow we understood one another with body language and mixed levels of English. On this train were young people from Turin, Barcelona, Seville, Salamanca, Murcia, England, Germany, a father-son duo from South Korea, and a young lady from Austria with whom I bonded immediately. She had just graduated from college, and had never been away from home. She was walking the Camino alone as I was, to challenge herself. I encountered her again on the road and received texts from her along the way.

I got lost in the Pyrenees. I set out with the others before light, impatient to get on the road on the first day. Stage 1 would take us from St. Jean Pied de Port in France to Roncesvalles in Spain. After Orisson, the halfway rest stop for lunch, I was falling behind and found myself walking alone. From Orisson, I estimated I had 14 km to Roncesvalles. I had walked almost 10 km when I noticed no one had appeared to overtake me on the road. My backpack was getting heavy and it was late in the afternoon. I knew by then I was off course. I concluded that I must be on the main road, in the same direction to Roncesvalles, instead of the walking path. I continued, hoping to get a road or Camino sign or to meet someone. But no one came along. I followed the narrow mountain road, paved with asphalt in some segments and loose gravel in others. I passed open farms with grazing cows. The road switched to a hairpin turn, which overlooked a steep beech forest. I heard bells, tied to sheep's necks. I then emerged into an open meadowland littered with smooth white boulders, where I thought Roncesvalles would be. To my dismay, I found a yellow arrow Camino sign pointing in the opposite direction.

I couldn't bear to go back 14 km to Orisson. I had walked eight hours in mountain terrain with a backpack and I was exhausted. I remembered having a phone number for the tourist information in Roncesvalles and thankfully, there was a cellular signal, so I called. What a relief when a live person answered and could speak a little English. She was so helpful and was able to figure out where I was from my description of the landscape. She said she'd send the red truck to pick me up, meaning the fire truck. I was horrified and told her just to send a taxi. It took about two hours for the taxi to arrive. The sun was setting and it was getting chilly, but I had everything in my backpack. I had a sleeping bag, half a sandwich left over from lunch and plenty of water. I peed in the open, made a nest with my backpack, relaxed and shut my eyes. I took in my surreal surroundings and listened to birds sing as they signaled where to roost. I drew my blanket close and I thought of Mama and Papa navigating the rugged Cordillera from Kalinga and imagined what it was like. Did they get lost too? Their walk was fraught with the danger of the Japanese advance. It was dark when the taxi arrived, and I had the driver call for a hotel en-route.

My friends asked if I was afraid, but I was not afraid at all. I felt I had the situation under control. If I can find a way to solve a problem, I don't get stressed, afraid, or worried. If the solution escapes me, I don't hesitate to draw others to help me. If I hadn't been able to reach anyone on the phone, I had planned to camp where I was for the night and see what help I could get in the morning. Or I could walk back to Orisson, refreshed after a good sleep. I felt safe. There were no wild animal predators in these mountains, and no one was there but me.

Stages 2 and 3 were arduous, mostly downhill, and very steep. The path was uneven with sharp edges, rock outcrops and paved with loose, irregular stones than could get slippery. My backpack was almost twenty pounds after loading water, ten pounds over the recommended weight. I had bruises on my arms from improper hoisting technique. The pressure and friction of the forward push on the toes from the downhill slope had already formed sore vesicles on my left foot. I had to stop numerous times to rest my knees, and to soothe my angry blister. Limping by now, I questioned my fortitude to walk the 27.4 km to Larrasoana. All I could think of at that time was putting one foot in front of the other and bearing the pain. After Larrasoana, the camino passes through Pamplona. I planned to explore Pamplona, made famous by Hemingway's "The Sun Also Rises" and taking the weekend off from the camino would give my expanding blister time to heal and allow a rendezvous with Aritz.

Aritz was an exchange student who lived with us twenty-five years ago when Doobie was in high school. We were so thrilled when we were reunited through Facebook the previous year. Aritz is Basque and he lived in Bilbao and was very near Pamplona, so we arranged a reunion. As soon as I completed the steep descent into Zubiri, a small village on the banks of Rio Arga, my blister was screaming so I called him to pick me up there instead of meeting in Pamplona which was still 5.5 km away. He came with his precocious nine-year-old daughter, very lively and outgoing, and beautiful. It was special to see him all grown up and to hear how he remembered his time with us fondly. We took a 42-km side trip south of Pamplona to the preserved medieval town of Olite, a national monument.

Gastronomy started in this region, rich in fresh products and shared wine production with the neighboring La Rioja. We indulged in tapas in the medieval square and a superb lunch in the Parador, the renovated old palace. In the evening we dined the Spanish way, very late and preceded by bar hopping for tapas and wine. Grilled *chuleta de ternera*, braised white asparagus, Navarre potatoes, and a salad of mixed garden vegetables, were all from the region and full of natural flavors.

After this indulgence I was back on the road. My blister had healed, and I relented and engaged a *mochila* (rucksack) transport service. A good decision, since Stage 4 , to Puente La Reina climbed steeply on a ridge, up to the wind turbines, then to the summit of Alto del Perdon, where there was a bronze memorial to pilgrims. The descent was on a rough and loose stone path to the Romanesque bridge over the Rio Arga, the Puente La Reina.

Stage 5 to Estella was peaceful, and the way moved along natural paths on gently rolling farmlands and vineyards. When I arrived in the town, they were on the fourth day of a weeklong fiesta. Everyone was costumed in white, with a red neckerchief. The squares were spilling over with partying locals eating, drinking, singing and dancing on the streets. In the main plaza there was a stage and a live band. In another, children's games were organized. A parade with drums and cymbals would burst out every so often, and there was a wall of chicken being roasted on stacked rotisseries. Chickens could only be purchased whole. The tables were communal, so I joined a group and shared my chicken and got the scoop on the fiesta. The revelry went on all night. My hotel was right on the square, so I couldn't sleep, and when at last sleep was possible after the music stopped at 4 am, I was awakened at 5 am by the rumble of garbage trucks. So I started later than usual. As my luck would have it, they were running the bulls that morning. It gave me a feel for what the more famous running of the bulls as written by Hemingway on the feast of San Fermin in Pamplona, was about.

Stage 6, to Los Arcos from Estella, was provocative because I'd heard about the fountains of wine along the way. It was true. The wine was flowing free from the spigots of Bodega Irache alongside the water fountains. Relaxed and fortified by wine, the Camino after this was over open farmlands, spread out on gently rolling hills, but offered little shade from the sun.

I wanted to experience communal accommodations, and to see for myself what the community of pilgrims was like, kicking their boots off at the end of a long day. Only those holding a pilgrim passport could book the *albergues*, or *refugios*. For eight to twelve euros one could get a bed space in dormitories for four or ten individuals with shared, segregated bathrooms. A few private rooms could be reserved, which I did, but it was a nuisance to get dressed just to go to the bathroom. The youth had more stamina. They socialized in the common areas, played cards, checked their hand held devices, watched sports, did laundry, or just hung out. Some read or updated their journals. I was exhausted and like me, the older pilgrims just ate dinner and crashed. After this experiment, I decided to stay in the most desirable accommodations in the area, and whenever there was a Parador I booked it, especially after I learned that pilgrims could get as much as 40% discount. Mama and Papa did not have these choices. They crossed rice paddies and depended on the kindness of poor barrio folks. They begged for shelter and for food. Later, this was impossible. At the height of the war people didn't trust each other. The Japanese confiscated harvest, so farmers hid their supply. Enemy collaborators infiltrated the farms and told on their neighbors.

Stage 7 from Los Arcos to Logronio was long, 28.8 km and over open lands that were exposed to the sun. I found out there was a bus leaving for Logronio that afternoon, and I decided to take it. I spent the day sitting in outdoor cafes watching locals come and go. I watched children play, and after exploring the narrow cobble streets I sat in the shade in the park. Town elders congregated there, socializing, reading the papers, and playing cards. My grandmother, Inay, indulged in a card game when I was a little girl in Pasacao. I walked over and they showed me how to play. It was very similar to Inay's *entre cuatro*. After watching them for a while, I visited the church where old women were occupied with chores helping the parish, cleaning, straightening the altar, and preparing pamphlets. *Deja vu*. My spinster aunts engaged in same volunteer work in their archdiocese. The small towns on the camino, one of which had just over fifty people, were surviving because of the pilgrims' business. Those not in their path, however, were dying. The population of these towns was old and stooped from osteoporosis, but it was amazing that their medieval villages were intact and they still lived in dwellings that their ancestors occupied. Something that couldn't be missed in these places was the church, the most impressive structure in any locality, and how religious rituals still governed the movements of life. This lifestyle had survived also in the Philippine barrios, a legacy of Spanish colonization.

I left the province of Navarre after Los Arcos for Logronio, the capital of La Rioja, the province named after the wine itself. Aritz joined me again to take me on a tour of its spectacular bodegas. Marques de Riscal was designed by Frank Gehry, of Bilbao's Guggenheim while Bodegas Ysios, by Calatrava, sat low on the plain, with undulating roof line that traced the silhouette of the Cantabrian mountains behind it. Alas, Bodega Antion, though architecturally impressive with its subterranean spaces and golden hue, was caught in the clutches of the economic collapse, abandoned with 30M Euro debt. In Haro, the wine capital, there were hundreds of bodegas. Its old town square was lined with tapas bars and wine cellars offering wine tasting. Aritz's great-grandfather had a winery and his grandmother inherited part of it, but at that time wine production was not the industry it is now, and she did not hold on to her share. Now Solabal, that winery, is a thriving, award-winning business run by his uncles. We stopped by for Aritz to collect his father's monthly supply and had a private tour and wine tasting with his uncle.

After arriving in Logronio on a bus, I embraced the idea that I could skip walking some stages so that I could make it to Santiago on my birthday, as I had originally planned. The pilgrimage was really shaping up to be My Way.

Instead of proceeding to Najera, Stage 8, I decided to take a detour. I asked Aritz to drop me off at San Millan de la Cogolla to visit the monasteries of Suso and Yuso, a World Heritage site. Dating back to the sixth century, it was the oldest monastic community in Europe. In Suso, with Visigothic, Mozarabe, and Romanesque characteristics, an anonymous monk first wrote down the Spanish language, Castellano. It was embellished later by the poet monk, Gonzalo Berceo. I thought this was profound. Today, after Mandarin and Hindi, Spanish is the third most widely spoken language in the world by native speakers. English is fourth, though it has the most global influence. I was determined more than ever, after this knowledge, to take my Spanish classes seriously. My basic skill in the language served me well in the Camino, but that was no longer enough for me. I stayed for the night in the luxurious Hospederia de San Millan, the converted monastery. The next day, I Googled the detour route to join the Camino again in Santo Domingo de la Calzada. On a picturesque stretch of checkered landscape, of vineyards, sunflowers and golden wheat, an old man walking to the next village stopped to chat. He asked me where I was from, shared stories about the Camino, and assured me I was walking in the right direction.

I skipped Stage 10-11 as the route to Belorado, in the province of Castilla Y Leon, followed the main road and offered little shade. Seeing Burgos was next, I mused, "Wouldn't it be befitting to arrive in Burgos on a horse? It is, after all, the land of El Cid."

I took the bus instead. This medieval World Heritage city was filled with architectural jewels, starting with its breathtaking gothic *Catedral de Santa Maria*. The second largest cathedral in Spain after Seville, it housed a wealth of art treasures and artifacts. I stayed two nights so I could take a side trip to Atapuerca, the excavation site of the *Homo Antecessor*. It is believed to be the oldest human species found in Europe, and there was ongoing archaeological research in the area.

There were so many sights to visit along the Camino, and upon discovering the many links to the Philippine's colonial past, in the food and lifestyle of these small villages, I became fascinated with the local history. It was a challenge to stay focused on the spiritual aspect of the journey.

From Burgos, the Camino entered the *Meseta*, the Spanish heartland. It was a long and seemingly endless stretch of high plains rimmed by mountains. The people of the *Meseta* were said to be ascetic and courageous. Touched with the mystical, visionary or madness, it inspired Cervantes in Don Quixote and shaped the likes of El Cid and the Saints and Mystics of the realm. Stage 15, from Castrojeriz in Burgos to Fromista, the Camino entered Palencia, which is also called the Tierra de Campos (Land of Fields). I descended from Castrojeriz and traveled on an old Roman road. I crossed the boundary at Rio Pisuerga on the medieval arched bridge, Puente de Itero. There was a delightful rest stop just before crossing the bridge. The 15th century Ermita de San Nicolas, converted into a hostel, was run by an Italian confraternity. It was without electricity and phones, but it had modern baths and toilets in a rear building. There were only twelve bed spaces, with breakfast and dinner served by candlelight.

The *Meseta* in summer was a waving golden landscape of shaved wheat fields against the horizon. Its roof was a clear blue sky that shimmered in the light. It was sublime, but it felt like eternity to cross on foot, and it offered no shade. Its tiny villages were scattered few and far between, and the journey was silent, with only the buzz of the 100F heat for company. Being Filipino, I knew about using umbrellas in the sun. Some *peregrinos* instantly embraced the idea, and followed suit.

It would have taken ten days to cover the *Meseta,* from Burgos to Astorga. I walked away from the sublime and jumped into a bus to Leon, skipping Stages 16-20. By this time my trek on the Camino was no longer a pilgrimage, but a travel odyssey.

It took some skill and asking around to get to these tiny and remote villages by the regional buses. No single bus line offered complete service, and I had to research which bus company stopped at my destination. Some villages didn't even have direct service, and I had to identify the connecting bus lines. To Leon, I had to take a connecting bus from Fromista, to Carrion de los Condes. It only had one weekly service, on Thursdays. How lucky could I be that the bus was scheduled to run that day? Otherwise, it would be a day's walk, 20.5 km. So I was in Carrion, waiting for the afternoon bus to Leon, and had time to kill. I wandered around the narrow and meandering streets of the village, and I came upon a plaque. It marked the birth home of Miguel de Benavides y Añoza (c. 1552–July 26, 1605), a Spanish clergyman and sinologist, the first Bishop of the Diocese of Nueva Segovia, the third Archbishop of Manila, and founder of the Universidad de Santo Tomas. If Mama had had less confidence in me, I would have enrolled in the University of Santo Tomas instead of the University of the Philippines. Serendipity indeed! I would discover these connections in other places as well, especially in Galicia and in the Basque country. Many Spanish sailors, adventurers and clergy sailed from these provinces for the Islas Filipinas in search of fortunes, souls to save, and fame. More than ever, I realized how deep the influence of Spain was in the Philippine culture.

Leon was a bustling metropolis that seamlessly combined the modern city with the magnificent artistic and architectural legacy of its long and storied past. Remnants of occupation by the Visigoths, the Romans, the Moors, and the Reconquista abound. Gaudi built a neo-Gothic palace here, Casa de Botines. It was the first monumental edifice constructed with secular and private funds rather than with religious or aristocratic patronage, and it represented a turning point in architectural practice. The city's museum of contemporary art, MUSAC, was housed in an avant-garde building and was holding an exposition on Spanish Femenismo. I stayed in the luxurious five-star Parador San Marcos, a former monastery and cloisters with a sumptuous Plateresque facade. The Rio Bernesga, spanned by its 16th century stone bridge, was visible from my window. The river was a recreation center among the Leonese. Families gathered at a picnic, strollers moved along the promenade, and anglers and colorful kayaks moved in the water. "I could easily live here," I mused. But I had also said that about Logronio.

I had to be in Santiago for my birthday, so I fast-forwarded to Astorga on a bus and skipped Stage 21-22.

Astorga is still rimmed by a medieval wall. Sitting on a ridge, it had spectacular views of the surrounding countryside. That weekend was pre-fiesta preparation for the weeklong celebration of the Festividad *de Santa Marta,* held on the last week of August. There were many events scheduled. Alas, Peter Blanchette, who was to appear at the Museo Romana de la Ergastula, was a no show for his baroque concert. More than thirty people were disappointed. Astorga, however, is the chocolate capital. with a Museo de Chocolate, so it was easy to get over the disappointment. I stayed at the Hotel Gaudi, in the shadow of the spectacular Gaudi Bishop Palace, which did not house any bishop, but the fascinating Museo de los Caminos. Dinner was the local specialty, *Cocido Maragato*. The *Maragato* tribe's numbers were dwindling, but this dish, very similar to the Philippine *puchero*, would live forever. It was a hearty, thick soup of garbanzos, cabbage, potatoes and seven kinds of meats that included chorizo, Iberian pig snout, ears and shoulder, chicken, smoked meat, beef meat or chops. According to tradition, each meat is served separately, and the meal finishes with soup.

After Astorga, the Camino begins to climb the mountains through the pass of Irago to their highest point at Cruz de Ferro, 4934 ft above sea level. I regretted bypassing this segment. I had wanted to deposit stones at the foot of this ancient iron cross to participate in the symbolic pilgrim ritual, but the route was described as arduous and the descent was steep and dangerous. Many pilgrim injuries were reported. Moreover, the way marks were said to be inconsistent and the weather unpredictable. And heading to O'Cebreiro, in Galicia, the climb was even steeper and more strenuous. The small villages in the mountains were just being reawakened to life by the resurgence of the Camino, and facilities for pilgrims were still sparse. I learned you can get to Sarria by train, and I made my decision. Remembering that I'd gotten lost in the Pyrenees, I was not inclined to test my luck so soon. Besides, this pilgrimage was now a travel adventure. I had become corrupted by the luxury that I allowed myself in the fine restaurants and five-star Paradors. I had separated myself from the community of pilgrims, who shared humble accommodations and suppers in *refugios*. I had lost my focus in seeking spirituality.

To be awarded a *compostela*, it is compulsory to walk the last 100 km from Sarria to Santiago on the French route. It didn't matter whether you had walked over 100 km before. I had walked 165.7 km at this point.

The Sarria segment was a very different Camino from the one that I started in St Jean Pied de Port. The town was terribly crowded with tourists, pilgrims, and backpackers, and the nonstop arrival of pilgrims has exhausted some of the local congeniality. I was rudely waved away and shooed when I tried to ask for directions to the Pilgrim's Office.

During the peak months of summer, around two-thousand pilgrims can arrive in Santiago daily. Many of them started in Sarria, to satisfy the requisite 100 km for a *compostela*. There were 183,366 pilgrims last year and during a Holy Year, when Saint James' feast on July 25 fell on a Sunday, the number doubled. Last was in 2010, and the next Holy Years would be 2021 and 2027.

There were big groups doing the Camino from Sarria, something I never saw from St. Jean. These were tourist groups, church groups, charity fundraising groups, youth groups, family reunions, organization groups, and a mass of young backpackers walking with a group of friends. The organized groups wore logo-ed matching T-shirts or hats, and carried very light daypacks as they had transportation support to ferry their luggage. They were talking non-stop and socializing, and obliviously, crowded me off the path. They laughed loudly, intruding on my silence. Gone was the camaraderie and fellowship between strangers who connect while engaged in mutual pursuits. Meanwhile, the young backpackers seemed to be in a hot race to get to Santiago. In the rest stops, these big groups occupied the place and inundated the service staff, displacing the lone walker. But it appeared everyone was having a good time and I decided to take the initiative and find out what these people were about. So maybe the Camino did something for me, despite my aloofness to its deeper tradition. My initial disapproval quickly dissipated. I did not get pissed off as I characteristically would have. I was okay with the idea that the Camino was for everyone. For whatever reason, and for whatever purpose one chose, the Camino is a unique and amazing experience. The Sarria segment may be a different Camino, but it doesn't make it the wrong Camino. For the record, the physical aspect of the Sarria route was a stroll in the park compared to St. Jean. The Galician countryside was a refreshing green landscape of rolling hills, farms and pastures. The mostly natural paths were in shaded woodland, tree-lined roads or under stands of eucalyptus.

I reached Santiago on August 23 in the mid-afternoon, setting out while it was still dark but taking it easy on the last day. Many aimed to reach the cathedral at noon for the pilgrim mass and walked at a furious pace. They came up from behind me with the sound of pounding boots, as if a stampede was approaching. Five km from Santiago, I climbed the hilltop at Monte de Gozo. On this summit the pilgrims since medieval times have gazed into the distance, and as the spires of the Cathedral came into view, they exclaimed gratitude and joy. The exhilaration was palpable in the throng, and I got swept up in it, too. I held the view in silence to contemplate the enormity of what the pilgrimage meant.

I was seeking spirituality, and I didn't know whether I achieved it or not. How did one experience it? I imagined it in medieval times. I looked back to when I had a Buddhist retreat in Tassajara. Was it achieving a state that born again Christians described? Was it the experience of mystics or religious converts? I went through many emotions, but often, I grieved for Mama and Johnny. They were the two most influential people in my life. Mama exerted her full power in shaping me, and I could see a lot of her in me, the full monty. She gave me the tools to make a life, and Johnny, made a full woman of me. Mama loved me, Johnny made me fall in love.

But there was still distance to cover before the cathedral. It seemed to take forever, slogging through the outskirts of the city on concrete pavement and crisscrossing with busy traffic until I reached Puerta do Camino, the gateway to the medieval city. I was really anticipating seeing the cathedral at this point, but it was elusive. As enormous as it was, I couldn't see it on the approach. But there were signs that it was ahead. The crowd in the squares started to swell, entertained by street performers. There was a string quartet playing Mozart, a couple doing a tumbling and juggling act, a bagpipe player, and living statues in costume. I arrived at a narrow and deep staircase tunnel. Its steps led into an opening to an immense square, and behold, the Cathedral of Santiago de Compostela!

Parador de los Reyes Catolicos, where I would be staying for the next three days, was right next to the Cathedral. On the square, the Plaza Obradoiro, was the whole world. There was a procession of chanting and saffron-clad Hare Krishnas. There were souvenir stands, pilgrims sprawled on the cobbled floor, tourists snapping pictures, and costumed medieval pilgrim pretenders. There was a long line at the cathedral steps, so I decided to check in to my hotel first and freshen up. Before I could unpack, a dozen red roses arrived from my sister Nancy for my seventieth birthday. How special!

Rested and showered, I proceeded to the cathedral to execute the pilgrim rituals. The Portico de Gloria and the Tree of Jesse were encased in scaffolding for restoration work, so I entered from a side door. I could peek to see the kneeling figure of Maestro Mateo in the back of the column. I couldn't touch my brow to his, and could only take a photo. I ascended to the High Altar, to the statue of St James, and touched his back and thanked him for my safe arrival and to bless all my loved ones. I descended to his crypt and paid my respects. Having missed the welcome Pilgrim mass at noon, I stayed for the four pm Pilgrim mass. Highlighting the ceremonial acts, one of the unique experiences in Santiago is to witness the *Botafumeiro*, the swinging of the giant incense burner during mass. It was no longer done regularly for each Pilgrim mass because it had become very expensive, costing 250 EU. It required eight attendants, or *tiraboleiros,* to control the path of the burner as it was swung across the aisle of the transept. Now it is only done on important holidays or when there is a request accompanied by a donation. Before I left Santiago, I returned to the Cathedral for the Pilgrim mass at noon, hoping to see the *Botafumeiro* lighted. I was not disappointed.

On August 25, my birthday, I took a bus to *Finisterre* to complete the Camino tradition. Believed to be the edge of the earth in medieval times, I watched the sun fall into the infinite sea, from *La Costa de Morta* (the Coast of Death). Meanwhile, in a distant cosmos, far, far away, Voyager 1 was approaching the edge of the solar system after thirty-five years of space travel.

I cheated and did the Camino my way. I completed its whole length of 800 km with buses and trains, and walked 269.7 km. I returned from the edge of the earth without achieving spiritual enlightenment, but with a clear head and with fresh vigor.

I had been married, had had children and grandchildren. I had a profession and a fulfilling career. I was financially independent. I had time to spend in pursuits that had been squashed earlier because life demanded other priorities. I was painting for pleasure. I was writing for publication. I was taking Spanish classes. I had returned to reading, which again was opening new worlds for me. I had become passionate about learning colonial history. I was traveling unfettered to all the magical places that I had dreamed about when I was a child. I was free! My cup runneth over. I'd been there, done that. I had accumulated material possessions. I did not lament downsizing to only the necessities. I was not wanting for anything. I was content. I lived alone, but I was not lonely. I was surrounded by family and friends. All of these, the Camino, My Way, clarified for me. It reminded me that the road I follow was my own, and that my choices made my life, and I am happy as I am.

> **"Never go on trips with anyone you do not love."**
> -Ernest Hemingway

CHAPTER 24: Misadventures in China - The Golden Girls' Grand Tour

August 2002

On the second week of our grand tour of China we decided to take a break at a McDonald's in Chengdu. We had just come down from Lhasa, Tibet, and we were hungry. Yak cuisine, I believe, is only cherished by yaks, and we had had enough Chinese food for a week, so we definitely needed a break. McDonald's was restorative. At an altitude of 13,000 feet, we had all gotten sick from the thin air with palpitations, shortness of breath, nausea, light-headedness, and terrible, pulsating headaches unresponsive to any analgesic. The only relief was to suck oxygen from aerosol canisters you could buy for 30 yuan, roughly $3.60. That's how I survived climbing the steep steps and breathing the thick incense of the Potala Palace.

My companions weren't so lucky. Tess was having palpitations during the climb and she didn't want to test the limits of her cardiac pacemaker, so she stayed in her bed. Didi tried to go out with me but she couldn't make the palace steps, so she decided to turn back and take refuge in the bus as it began to rain torrents accompanied by whipping winds. Myrna came down with the flu when we left Xian, so she also had fever and chills on top of altitude sickness. She only saw her bed and the bowl of the toilet during the two days we spent in Tibet. She didn't eat for two days and was glad to lose weight, her only consolation. She was so worried while she was ill that she agreed to see the hotel doctor. He made a room call, gave her a physical, confirmed she had the flu and altitude sickness, and then gave her a shot and a supply of medicine all for Y 100, the equivalent of $12.60. She said she would return to see the sights she missed only if she was crazy.

From the start, this Golden Girls' 60th birthday bash was already full of misadventures. Didi narrowly escaped missing boarding our flight in Vancouver. She was delayed because she had to step out of the security area and arrange for her camera to be put in checked baggage. She forgot to load the batteries and therefore could not operate the camera for inspection. Meanwhile Tess' luggage did not show up on arrival in Beijing which forced us to go shopping for necessities before our guide could join us to translate. It was hilarious as we tried to ask where to buy lingerie by miming putting on a bra and panties. Thankfully her suitcase arrived after a couple of days, but within that time Didi's camera which survived customs inspection, got lost in her hotel room.

We couldn't wait to explore Beijing. Beijing was venerable, ancient and impressive. It was hosting the 2008 Summer Olympics and you can't not know about it for all the street hawkers pushing Olympic-logo-ed hats and stuff. You think everything in Texas is big? Well, Tiananmen Square holds one million people. I can't even imagine that. And it requires aerobic fitness and good running shoes to traverse. The Forbidden City is forbiddingly huge as well, with one courtyard after another and another. Just to get from room to room is like walking to the next block. Underneath its floors are six meters of stone to prevent enemies from tunneling in. It had no trees, for similar enemy-deterring reasons. Barren and forbidding indeed!

Beijing is over 2000 years old, as most of the other places we explored. On visiting these ancient cities on our 60th birthdays, why, we felt practically girlish!

I lost the group in the Temple of Heaven and wandered into the surrounding gardens amidst 600-year-old cypress trees. I thought it was there where I felt most the intention of the Temple and was meant for me to experience. It was like the uplifting one feels in the solemn, soaring space of cathedrals. I was thinking that should I fail to rejoin the group I'd just take a taxi to the hotel. But Peter, our tour manager, found me.

You'd think it would be smooth sailing from here on, but no!

We checked in for a very early flight to Xian, still groggy from lack of sleep because we had played mahjongg until 2 am and barely had enough time to repack and make it to the airport. Playing mahjongg in hotels is easy in China. Everybody does it in their rooms, and every hotel is equipped with tables and mahjongg sets to rent by the hour. I bought an exquisite hand-carved black agate mahjongg set and we used it to play that second night in Beijing, only to discover that the set was the mainland version, not the familiar Hong Kong set we are used to. Mainland mahjongg has eight fewer flower tiles, and I regrettably had to return the set.

Well, our flight was delayed for four hours. But China Southern was customer friendly. They booked all the passengers at a nearby hotel, gave us full breakfasts, and told us to rest and take a nap and they'd ring us when our flight was ready.

Xian was lovely. Our hotel faced the city square and every morning at first light, everyone comes out for Tai Chi. There are no health clubs, so the citizens use public spaces for these activities and for social gatherings. There was a group of women who exercised with colorful fans and another group with a leader who called out the graceful, sustained movements to hypnotic music. With the morning light coming in at an angle against the ancient city walls and reflecting over the Drum and Bell Towers, the whole scene was mesmerizing, surreal. In neighborhood alleys, people played chess and mahjongg, did each other's hair, washed the baby or brushed their teeth, socializing simultaneously. And of course the famous terra cotta warriors were just mind-boggling. The imagination of this particular Qin Dynasty emperor was truly beyond ordinary. The Big Wild Goose Pagoda paled in comparison. However, disaster! We didn't have enough time to do shopping. Our local guide, Margaret, was very proud of her city and was determined to give us the experience she thought we required to appreciate her city. She was a hard taskmaster and exhorted us against shopping for bargains and fakes, and warned us not to fall for ruses and manipulations by these new capitalists. In the end Margaret was right, and we enjoyed her city the most thanks to her.

After Xian, our flight to Lhasa, Tibet was uneventful, but our acquaintance with the city was a blur.

As soon as we descended from Lhasa to Chengdu, we felt much better. The headaches just disappeared. After McDonald's, we were off to Chongqin, where we would board the boat that would take us to the Yangtze River for a three-day cruise. We would be passing through the Three Gorges, which next year will disappear in the biggest dam project in the world. When the dam is operational, the water will rise to 145 meters and will flood the ancient towns and cultural relics on its banks. When May, our local guide announced that we have a four-hour bus ride to Chongqin and that we should all head for the bus station already, we all cracked up. It triggered recall of popular Filipino word play jokes about our English pronunciations. Right away I yelled to Myrna, "Hey, use devastation in a sentence". And on cue Myrna replied, "to go to Chongqin, pirst we must go to de-bas-tey-shon". We doubled over laughing, and I'm sure the other folks on the tour group thought we had all gone mad. We went on and on with "Hey, use tenacious in a sentence". "I put on my tey-na-shus, before going out to play", and so forth, until we exhausted our repertoire.

A cruise on the Yangtze is not anything like going on a Disney Big Red Boat. There is absolutely nothing to do but sit and watch the scenery. We went on off-shore excursions to ancient temples built on the sides of the mountain plunging into the river. We took a ski lift to the Ghost City, sited atop the summit and full of torture chambers and scary monsters and grotesque mythical creatures. It was where sinners were sent to be purified for reincarnation. We paddled upstream in tributaries and reached pristine blue-green crystal waters enveloped by soaring mountain walls on each side. It didn't take long to discover the art of doing nothing. It was actually peaceful. In the evenings it was mahjongg time until Didi and Myrna got on each other's nerves and began wagging fingers in each other's faces and getting worked up over nothing. We quit mahjongg right then and there and didn't touch it again. But we love each other, so the next day all was forgiven and we prepared for the eagerly- awaited sojourn to Shanghai. With mahjongg banned for the rest of our trip, I wasn't able to recover my loss of $60.

Shanghai is Chicago along the "Bund," New York along the East Bank, and China in the Old Town. It has the pulse of the West, with frenetic shopping on Nanjing Road and gleaming, breathtaking skyscrapers in the new city that rose from the East Bank marshes only in the last ten years. Its sweeping highway exchanges put Atlanta's Spaghetti Junction to shame, and the tallest communication tower in the world gives its skyline a futuristic ambience. We found a bottle of French Bordeaux, that was past its prime, and drank to my 60th birthday. It was Sunday, the 25th of August in Shanghai, the city that conjures mystery, intrigue and forbidden pleasures for many in the West.

The next day we were back to reality. We were going home, and suddenly we couldn't wait to get going. The Pacific crossing was so long, and we needed to stay overnight in Vancouver to get a flight home to Atlanta very early the next day. But that was OK, for as soon as we got into Vancouver's spanking new international concourse we were grateful for the clean and deodorized restroom facilities with soap and paper supplies and flushing seat toilets. We never got used to the crouching position and the heavy stink of open floor urinals without flushing water and toilet paper in China. Flushing seat toilets are the hallmark of advanced civilization, don't anybody dispute that! We couldn't stomach another Chinese meal, so we went to Goldilocks and feasted on Filipino kare-kare, binagoongan, dinuguan, and sago drink. All was well, and we would be home soon. Or so we thought. Our connecting flight from Minneapolis had been canceled and Northwest was going to put us on their last flight out of there three hours later. Unacceptable! Our graciousness and equanimity had been spent in China. We demanded to be booked on another airline at their expense, immediately. We landed at Hartsfield on Delta only forty minutes later than our original scheduled arrival with all our luggage and pasalubong intact. We were home!

CHAPTER 25: Turkey Trot

April 22-May 10,2010

My classmate Josie had been hosting a travel group from Buffalo for many years and I knew many of her followers. I was the newest of her recruit and with fifteen of us, dubbed the Olympians after Josie's surname, we were the majority in this tour group of twenty-nine. For such a large group we got along very well. We should know how to behave, after all, most of us have already qualified for Medicare. It is very likely, however, that our exemplary behavior was shaped by our program director, Serif, who led the tour with the precision and discipline of an army sergeant and the erudition of a professor, of which he was both in another life. He is proud of his country and its history and we're incurable romantics, so we were easily charmed and won over. We loved the tales about Tamel, a beguiling figure of humor who knows not to sweat life's details, and eagerly awaited our daily installment.

Turkey is an amazing land and visiting it brings to life the history of the world which in high school made for a dreary class that involved memorizing dates and wars. Turkey indeed is a crossroad of civilization and this educational and cultural tour conveyed that vividly, but what's breathtaking is the transformation of a nation gestated from centuries of imperial sectarian rule and birthed from a bloody war into a modern secular republic. With Ataturk's leadership it brought about legal, social, and economic reforms that propelled the country into the 21st century in a generation. The father of the republic is beloved in Turkey, and his name is spoken in reverence, a larger than life figure, Mustafa Kemal Ataturk.

We'd start our day with Tamel. His antics kept us alert and set our mood right. Serif ran a tight schedule and packed a lot of stuff in a day. He was determined to enrich our experience and educate us about Turkey, and he even gave us a quiz at the end of the tour and graded our paper! Here's a Tamel tale: Tamel just became a new father and his neighbor asks him, "What did you have, a boy or a girl?" He answers, "A boy." "So what's his name?" the neighbor asks. And Tamel answers, "I don't know, he can't talk yet".

Our tour started in Istanbul and immediately we were hooked. From the airport on our way to the hotel in Taksim Square, we drove along the coast of the Sea of Marmara, then the Golden Horn, its banks lined with parks and promenades and bursting with multi-hued tulips. The tulip originated from Turkey. The flower is featured in ancient carpets, ceramics, and art, but flourished in Holland after it was exported there by a British diplomat. Istanbul is reclaiming it by staging a Tulip Festival in spring and planting millions of the bulb annually. It's simply awesome to know that the city sits on two continents, Europe and Asia, and the narrow Bosphorus Strait that separates them connects two bodies of water, the Sea of Marmara and the Black Sea. We were out early one morning and it startled us to see dolphins bobbing in and out of the water in the middle of a bustling city with Russian oil tankers on its way to the Black Sea. I don't know what to make of Istanbul. It has the romance of the past, it was once Constantinople. It has magnificent antiquities, the Blue Mosque, Hagia Sophia, Topkapi Palace, Dolmabahce Palace. Its new high-rises grow among ruins of Roman rule, underground cisterns, aqueducts, and the hippodrome. It is Asia with the Egyptian Spice market and the grand bazaar, it is Europe with outdoor cafes and the ballet and opera, and its grand houses and mansions along the Bosphorus. It is bustling with commerce along the Golden Horn and Taksim Square is lined with restaurants and pubs. But the country, though secular, is 99% Muslim and the chanting call for prayers five times a day is announced from minarets that pierce the skyline like standing sentinels. This might be odd to a Christian, but what about a Muslim who is jolted by church bells tolling?

One doesn't see the burqa, but many women young and old still wear the scarf and keep themselves covered, and some men still wear the fez. I can imagine some identity confusion in the young generation that would be akin to the ambivalence and cultural dilemma faced by children of immigrants from southeast Asia in the USA. Unless you're in touristy areas, ordering a drink can be a challenge, and pork is not part of the cuisine.

Aah, the cuisine, I could eat it every day, especially the eggplant dishes and the cold appetizers, and I love lamb, so it's a feast. The kebabs are seasoned so well and very tasty, grilled to tenderness. Baklava originated from Turkey, but somehow the Greeks attached it to themselves and marketed that to the world. There is an infinite variety of flavors of baklava, and each one packs calories, but who cares? I loved the lahmahcun, a flat, thin-crust dough painted with sweet tomato paste and cheese or ground meat on top, baked in a stone oven then garnished with parsley and sprinkled with fresh lemon juice, rolled and eaten immediately. It melts in your mouth. I discovered a new fruit, too, which I had every day for breakfast, the loquat, and I developed a taste for halva, a silky semolina and sesame paste confection mixed with nuts and honey. We had a cooking demonstration by Sahin, a renowned Antalya chef, and I will adapt his halva for my dinner guests, with an extra Metty flourish.

We crossed the Dardanelles from European Turkey to Asian Turkey, moving along the coast of the Sea of Marmara. In Galipoli, we stopped to ponder the human tragedy of war. Turkish troops led by Ataturk defeated the ANZAC forces of the Allies here in WWI with heavy casualties on both sides, about 250,000 each. We arrived the day after the anniversary of the battle, and there were still fresh flowers on the graves.

Surrounded by politically unstable countries, Turkey maintains a large compulsory armed forces. It has Syria, Iraq and Iran on its southeast border, Armenia and Georgia to the northeast, Russia over the Black Sea, and Greece and Bulgaria in the northwest. It has been invaded through the centuries from all directions, and its current real estate has been carved through war. Its recent revolutionary past is fresh in the nation's mind, so serving in the force is an honor and carries much prestige. A young man's lack of service credentials could be a deal breaker in applying for jobs or in marriage.

Asian Turkey is Anatolia, in Asia Minor in ancient times, in the Fertile Crescent, and it shared epochal events with other legendary lands like Mesopotamia, Persia, Baghdad, Palestine, Jerusalem, Egypt, Greece, and Rome, where god-like men ruled, where Suleiman the Magnificent and Alexander the Great built empires. Homer hailed from Turkey. There are many Christian sites in Turkey. The Virgin Mary retired in Ephesus after Jesus' crucifixion. Mt. Ararat of Noah's fame is in Turkey. St Paul did his conversion in Turkey and addressed the Seven Churches of the Revelation. There's the Basilica of St. John and his tomb. Christians fled to Cappadocia from Roman persecution and carved living spaces and churches in the Tufa formations, where their magnificent frescoes still shine brilliantly today.

These people left behind self-contained cities underground that are nine stories deep and which protected inhabitants from enemies with stocks of animals, provisions, and even wine making facilities. Cappadocia is incredible with fanciful tufa formations that look like fairy chimneys, or if you're really imaginative, they look like penis heads in an obscene valley of white undulating mountains. We glided over this surreal landscape at sunrise in a hot air balloon. In Pamukkale there are hot springs and white travertine pool terraces that defy description. You can even swim in a pool littered with ancient artifacts and fed by hot springs. Turkey has an esteemed past, and excavations throughout Turkey document its history and this rich yield of artifacts fill their antiquities museum and tell the story of man himself. The great civilizations of the ancient world had a foothold in Turkey, from the Chalcolithic period eons ago to the modern republic, they marched along through their golden apex until their destruction by conquest or nature's ire. The Hittites, Lydians, Lyceans, Phrygians, the Hellenistic and Roman outposts, Troy, Byzantium, the Seljuks, the Celts, and the Ottoman Empire; we visited the remains of all these civilizations and imagined what they were like.

In Izmir, we had a home visit in Gobeller, a small village of 100 families where the family spoke no English and we spoke no Turkish, but we managed and had a great time. We were in groups of five, and I was with the group who had lunch with Birol and his family. He is a tractor operator from what we can gather, has a pretty wife who was very sweet and proudly served us lunch using her good matching dinner set. She had two daughters ages six and three, and the latter was at home and the cutest ever. The older girl was in school. We visited a village one-room school teaching grades 1-3, and a fourth grade classroom in another school in a larger town. All the school children wear a uniform, and they are excited to have their pictures taken and to speak English. They were happy and open and spontaneous. Children are special in Ataturk's vision, they have a National Children Holiday. The student, the farmer, and the soldier are the vessels to the future for this young republic.

We covered great distances on this tour and it was crucial to have timely pit stops. Serif was cognizant of that and in every stop he gave information to the toilets first thing, and we learned very quickly that you have to ask for directions to the water closet WC, not the ladies room, and *bayan* is girl and *girin* means enter. In some you must pay a Lira to use it, and there's no guarantee whether you get a sit-down commode or an Asian squat-hole, or if there's toilet paper provided. Some were not able to do it squatting and were forced to queue for a long time for the limited seat commode. Despite this, bathing remains an art in Turkey, and the famous Turkish bath in Cannakale was a great discovery for me. I was scrubbed and washed and covered with suds, then laid out nude on a warm marble platform under a skylight in a coed bath with two young and gorgeous Turks on each side. How much more exciting Turkey can be?

Our flight back home was canceled due to the ashes still being blown by Iceland's Eyjafjallajokul volcano. I was rebooked to Chicago from Istanbul, and system computer glitches caused verification delays which almost caused us to miss flight connections. We had to sprint to board and in Chicago I had to recheck my luggage myself from Terminal 5 to Terminal 2, and get them up and down the train with only twenty minutes to make it. I was almost denied boarding, but luckily I'm a platinum Skymiles member so I was upgraded to first class. Phew! I ordered Patron as soon as I was seated.

So here's Tamel on his first flight, he was going to the Black Sea. He got on board and sat in the First class cabin even though his ticket was economy. He wouldn't budge after the stewardess repeatedly requested him to transfer so she called the pilot to handle the matter. The pilot, recognizing Tamel's origins from his attire, whispered something in his ear and promptly Tamel got up and transferred to the economy cabin. The stewardess, impressed asked the pilot what he whispered in Tamel's ear. The pilot said, "Oh, I just told him that the seat he was on wasn't going to the Black Sea, and that it was in the next cabin."

CHAPTER 26: Island Fantasies, No Man Is An Island

November 3, 2002

What is it about Islands that beckon? I suppose each of us can come up easily with our own vision of island living. I grew up in the Philippine Islands, and know exactly what it's like to live in an island, and so I wonder what possessed me to pay $450 a day to stay at Greyfield Inn on Cumberland Island where there's absolutely nothing but maritime wilderness. The only lodging in town is Greyfield Inn with twelve rooms; otherwise you backpack and rough it in the wilderness camps to sleep over on the island. Greyfield is a 5-star historic inn operation where dinners are a dressed-up affair preceded by cocktails and civilized conversation in the antique-furnished living room, and where you are given a tour of the Island by a resident naturalist in an open truck with blankets provided to warm your lap. At the end of the tour, he switches the wheels to the 4-wheel mode and drives on the beach for miles, and you see nothing but wide dune-scapes and wild horses and shore birds and foaming waves under a sunlit blue sky. The air meeting your face is crisp and fresh you can just feel the exchange of gases taking place in your lungs: clean air in, polluted city air out. After the tour, you can pick up your gourmet picnic basket and you can take it anywhere to have lunch. You can eat in the wide front porch, on picnic tables on the front lawn, or in the back overlooking the marsh. If you're feeling adventurous, you can take it under the canopies of spreading live oaks decorated with hanging Spanish moss, or to the beach on a towel spread on sugar-white sand.

On the beach you can walk for miles without meeting anyone except a wild horse or a flock of migrating swallows or sea gulls. The inn provides special bikes you can ride on the sand, and I learned to ride the bicycle this way, an exhilarating experience I'll always treasure for years to come. Camping out means, well, you know what camping is. It would be not as primitive if you could get reservations in the Sea Camp area, the only developed section of the island available to the public. For $4 a day, plus the $12 ferry ride to get to the island, you can have camping amenities such as a power connection, flushing toilets, cold showers, and fire pits for cooking. But you have to bring everything else, of course, and carry it on your back for at least five and a half miles. And then you pack all your garbage after breaking camp and take it on your back again because you're supposed to leave the place undisturbed, without any sign that you've been there. Cars are not allowed on the Island unless you're a descendant of the original landowners, who still owns 10% of the island. The rest of the island is owned and administered by the Park Service as a National Seashore. That was designated in 1972 after wrangling by conservationists, developers, politicians, and the heirs of industrial tycoons, primarily the Carnegies who owned the island after the British left. Now the Island belongs to the public, albeit in limited ways. Because it is operated as a wilderness area there are restrictions on its use. The four camp sites, three of which are in wilderness areas, only accept twenty reservations each at a time for a maximum of seven days each stay, so the island only sees about 50,000 visitors a year. The waiting list is about six months. It is the same for Greyfield Inn, the only remaining private enterprise on the Island by virtue of inheritance. If the owners decide to sell, the National Park Service has first option on the property, which it will exercise for sure so that the whole island will eventually be public.

I made reservations a year ago only to cancel because Johnny was stricken with virulent systemic lupus. When he got well enough to travel, I made another reservation to visit the Island to celebrate our 34th wedding anniversary. I mentioned this to friends during dinner at home one night and all at once everyone wanted to come too. Right then and there we logged on the Inn website, and as fate would have it there were three rooms available, and the Abelleras, Mallaris, and Apanays booked them that very instant.

Why did we want to go? Why all this excitement about an Island? The first time I returned to visit home, after being away for twenty years, we went to a resort island off of Cebu. It was a different experience from what I had when I was growing up in Pasacao. Though those childhood years in Pasacao I remember as priceless, the island experience this time as an adult has other yearnings and fantasies tacked on to it. Perhaps I have been influenced heavily already by western ideas, and have drifted far from my roots. I said then, "Oh, let's buy a little Island here to retire to!" And what was I envisioning? I had an image of an idyllic paradise with sunshine and balmy weather all year round, fragrant breezes blowing my hair, walking barefoot on the beach under moonlit skies. I saw myself, the queen of this piece of earth, separate from the rest of the world, self-sufficient and beholden to no one. I would surround myself with beauty and with the joyous company of family and friends, who would come and visit and be showered with my hospitality.

That was the scenario. I thought it was original until I learned about the settlers of Cumberland Island, especially the last tycoons who built their mansions there and tried to live on the island, albeit more grandly, but the broad stroke is exactly as I saw it in my whimsical musing.

The island belonged to the Timucuan Indians in pre-Columbian times. They are now extinct, killed by the diseases brought by the European colonists, against which these tribes had no immunity. They were tall, reaching seven feet to the Spaniards' five and a half. They were formidable and brave warriors to be sure, but the white man's germs wiped them out, and a succession of these white settlers tried to live on the island. When the English drove out the Spaniards, they named the

Island after the Duke of Cumberland. Later the Crown parceled the island out to loyal subjects and the Island evolved its plantations until they were broken up after the Civil War. The new industrial tycoons, the Carnegies primarily, bought most of the acreage and tried to live their fantasies on the island in much the same way I envisioned it.

The Dungeness Mansion and surrounding gardens, which are now in ruins, was the center of that lifestyle. It hosted glittering socials for family and VIPS and the beautiful people of the era. It cultivated crops and raised farm animals, it fished in the surrounding waters, it was a self-sustaining entity. But it didn't last. The dream could not be sustained. The ill-fated John Kennedy Jr. and Carolyn Bissett had very romantic notions of the Island and had their supposedly secret wedding there. Today the Island is close to how it was when the Timucuans boiled the hallucinogenic sap from the indigenous holly bushes that grow on the North Shore for use in their rituals. So our company of dear friends drank Cabernet Sauvignon that we smuggled in our luggage, we toasted our affection for one another, cherished our fortune of being together as couples for over thirty years, and we got to live our island fantasies for the daily price of $450. That was a good deal if we forget about the swarm of ticks and gnats and mosquitoes that would eat one alive whenever the air got warm. At the end of it, we were glad to flee the island in a fast boat.

CHAPTER 27: There's Wine in Them Thar Hills

In fancy company, we like to think of ourselves as oenophiles. But among kin and friends, we are viewed as a bunch of pretenders who get drunk and silly on a scheduled basis. So every month we have dinner in each other's homes and introduce personal wine discoveries to accompany the food. For the most part, our search would take us to Dekalb Farmer's Market or Costco, or World Markets, to browse their wine ratings and check the bargains. But some of us who are retired and can take off anytime to travel have gone for wine pilgrimages to the hallowed and ancient lands of vinification in Italy and France and to the nouveau lands of Sonoma and Napa Valleys. In all of these the delight is in outdoing one another in displaying one's wine tasting vocabulary, never mind that we have no idea on how to judge the wine. But then, just like beauty is in the eye of the beholder, good wine is in the palate of the imbiber, a matter of personal taste.

This is the only way to view the exercise if we are to keep our affection for one another. Otherwise it would be an oenologist's war, for each one of us is passionate when we describe how a particular vintage affects us. We can wax poetic with our tongues, describing a particular wine's bouquet, or legs, or sweetness, or dryness, or it's finish or nose. Sometimes the descriptions can become X-rated, particularly when you're searching for the subtlest nuance to convey a wine's body. Do you notice how consistent wine's imagery is with seduction? If you close your eyes and listen to a wine's description, you'd think one is describing a full-bodied voluptuous woman with a fresh grass smell and great legs and ruby or cranberry red lips with an apple or musky aftertaste! You would notice in this particular group too, with an aggregate of 145 married years among them, how the talk easily descends into the gutter after the first few bottles are uncorked. The descriptions become wild, then crude, as boys who've had a few are wont to do. But since their tongues are now nimble and loose, and the grape's nectar is in the head, we learn of secrets that help them to stay the virile boys that they are. So we look at them with indulgence and generosity and refrain from washing their mouths with soap.

The year before, we decided to mark our anniversaries of marital togetherness in Cumberland Island, and the fond memories still linger and are reviewed every time we meet. We note that I learned how to ride the bicycle there on the pristine white beach, witnessed by shore birds and wild horses, fear of falling easily whisked away by the gentle reassurance of friends and the exquisite peace bestowed by the tranquil island that still exists as god intended it to be. This year, we decided to go to the mountains and witness fall in its splendor. A friend offered the use of his mountain retreat nestled on a hill along the banks of the Chestatee River.

But what can one do in Dahlonega, Lumpkin County? Is there any restaurant one can dine in? What can we do to fill the time? Once you've viewed the scenery, what is there to do? We look down on the Chestatee as we swing on the wide back porch. We supposed we could go fishing, but it's past the fishing season and the fish are gone. From March to September the Chestatee obliges anglers with rainbow and brown trout, spotted, white and redeye bass, stripers, bluegill, and redbreast. But it's now November. Our cook (who we brought along, fearing we'd find no place to dine in the mountains) ventured to get in the water and cast a fishing pole, but only caught thumb-sized specimens not fit for the grill.

So we thought of other things to do. In the summer one can float down the Chestatee on rafts and ride the white rapids, or view the falls that drop about 60 feet along the river's way. This river's headwaters spring from Lumpkin County and meander along valleys and hills before emptying into Lake Lanier. It is the little brother to the mighty Hooch. In some sections, the river bottom had been defaced by dynamite blasting, and river rocks and boulders were disturbed from their natural state by men prospecting for gold in the Dahlonega quarries, the site of the first US gold rush in the 1800's. Did you know that there was once a mint in Dahlonega to strike those gold US coins? You can learn all about the first gold rush in the USA in the Gold Museum in Dahlonega and visit a gold mine and pan for gold, if that's your thing. But our thing is shopping, so we set out to the historic town square where there are several antique emporiums filled with treasures as good as gold. My shopping coup is a wine cork bulletin board with pewter wine-themed push pins, a marvelous souvenir of our expedition!

We discovered there is wine in them thar hills! Because of its elevation, about 1600-1800 feet above sea level, and the cooler temperatures, the north Georgia mountains are hospitable to growing certain varieties of grapes, notably cabernet francs and merlots. There are dedicated oenophiles and vintners, who for the sheer love of vinification, staked out their fortunes in these mountains, and just like the early prospectors for gold, they dug into the ground to find their treasure. Today, they are pouring their initial vintages from the barrels and producing wines that are gaining attention from the big boys and attracting audiences like us from established wine-tasting touring centers such as Napa and Sonoma. They have formed cooperatives and market a wine trail tour. We visited Three Sisters Vineyards. The name was inspired by the spectacular view of the three mountain ranges straddling the tri-state border of Tennessee, North Carolina, and Georgia, just a hop and a skip away from our cottage on the Chestatee. They have uncorked their 2001 Meritage wines, so named because of their merit and heritage. Accompanying it were fine handcrafted cheeses from Sweet Grass Dairy Farms in Thomasville, Georgia. We sampled Botana, an aged goat cheese which won second place in the American Cheese Society

Competition, and a cheddar, Clayburne, which won first place in the cow cheese category.

Our hosts during the wine tasting were the owners, Doug and Sharon Paul, who craft their wines with love and pride and also collect fine handcrafted jug pottery indigenous to the region. Their Meritage Merlot won first place in the Wine Spectator's ratings of Georgia wines in 2003. The wine trail lists several wineries; Frogtown Cellars, Wolf Mountain Vineyards, Habersham Vineyards, Crane Creek, Chestnut Mountain Winery, Chateu Elan, Fox Vineyards, Split Rail, Tiger Mountain, Puckett Family Vineyards, Georgia Wines, and Persimmon Creek. Napa Valley, watch out!

We went to the mountains to be away and to be together and to enjoy food and wine.

Our first night we had Italian sausage spaghetti marinara, accompanied by Italian wines, a fine Barolo and Riserva Chianti among the four bottles we consumed. The second night, we had grilled pork loins accompanied by various pinot noir from California, Chile and France. In between, during snacks and mahjong, we finished off a beaujoulais, a merlot, Spanish and Argentinian reds, and a German riesling. Evening entertainment was mahjong, and to have a quorum we needed Eudy to play, but she didn't know the game and she demurred from learning. She whined and complained, and protested, but she was given a proposal she couldn't refuse, (we'd play Scrabble with her) and so she learned the game and played to complete the women's quorum, albeit with the coaching of our cook who was at her side throughout. Our cook is a skilled player, so it must be Eudy's luck that determined her position as the sole loser after two nights of play. We felt guilty taking her money, but she was not spared. Mahjong is mahjong, we take no prisoners!

We dined in during our stay but on our way back home a lunch stop at the historic Smith House was a must. An endless stream of juicy fried chicken, roast beef, ham, vegetables and side dishes are served throughout, with a peach cobbler a la mode to finish the meal. Yummy! We parted at Smith house after the belly-busting all-you-can-eat lunch. But for the golfers, the day had just begun with a tee time at Gold Creek, the Robert Trent Jones complex on Hwy 136. I shot a 97, a perfect conclusion to a wonderful weekend. The bacchanalia of food and wine, mahjong and laughter rising above the rumble and swish of the Chestatee will bring fond memories for many months as we consume our supply of Three Sisters 2001 Cabernet Franc, until the next year's get-away.

CHAPTER 28: Grouper Omelette

Bring seven friends over for a seafood night at the beach.

Start with Dom Perignon 1993 and Brillat Cheese from Star Provisions.

Follow with a fine 1993 Barolo, a voluptuous 1994 Brunello and a silky Cabernet.

Serve colossal steamed fresh red shrimps from the gulf, seared glazed scallops, assorted seafood & spinach stew, grilled vegetables, and a huge grilled grouper

Finish with rum cake and Grand Marnier and Remy Martin Champagne Cognac XO.

Go to bed and wake up groggy and watch the sunrise with your morning java cuppa.

Flake a fistful of the left-over grilled grouper.

Combine with chopped left-over sliced tomato from the meal before last.

Scrounge for left-over mango and onions and chop.

Heat a non-stick pan with 1 tbsp oil.

Beat 4 eggs and set aside.

Sauté the flaked grouper with the chopped ingredients

Spread solids evenly on the pan when the onions are wilted .

Pour the egg over and let the underside set over medium heat.

Take a plate and balance it over the pan.

With a flick of the wrist and an excess of confidence, turn the pan over the plate.

Slide the inverted omelet back to the pan and finish cooking until the opposite side is set.

Go back to your coffee and let the others cook the rest of breakfast.

Bon Appetit!

CHAPTER 29: Music To My Ears, In the Footsteps of Ravel and Debussy

I was thinking I'd share the treats I enjoyed on this trip with my friends as soon as it was my turn to host dinner. By the time I completed the tour, I had the whole evening planned. The house will glow with candle light and will smell of lavender from the hills of San Sebastian. I will await their arrival with Ravel's "Le Tombeau de Couperin", and greet them with his "Jeux D'eau". I'd switch to Debussy's "d'Images" during cocktails, and I'll pour my prunelle and pomme liqueur aperitifs from Navarre, serving hors d'oeuvres of aged goat cheese and shaved monk's head cheese from the Basque region. And of course foie gras with sauterne will be on the cocktail table, too. Perhaps duck will be the main entrée, and dessert could be the easy confection described by my new gourmand friend from Indiana: puff pastry filled with fresh raspberry marinated in Grand Marnier and a sprinkle of sugar, topped with real whipped cream. Yummm! That would go with another Basque liqueur, the honeyed and herbed armagnac, and then I'd finish the meal off with coffee and chocolates from Foucher's of Paris. For the meal I'd pick some good Bordeaux from my favorite sommelier, the Dekalb Farmer's Market. Under the influence of these distilled nectars of the grape, my guests will be a captive audience and will indulge me as I recall the pleasures of this last trip.

"What is more beautiful than a road?", asked George Sand, aka Amandine Aurore Lucie Dupin, baronne Dudevant, 19th century French novelist and feminist. For nine years she was Chopin's lover and muse. She is just one of the many colorful personalities I've discovered on this Spanish-French quest to understand the lives and music of Ravel and Debussy.

My concert pianist friend from Baltimore, Linda, had been asking me to join her in one of the musical tours she'd been taking for the past five years. Most of the participants, I've learned, have been coming for the last seven to nine years and have come to know each other like old friends. Of the thirty four participants, twenty are music professionals, either as pianists or teachers, or serious piano students. My own musical background consisted of inventing clever ways of avoiding piano practice or dodging piano lessons from the stick-wielding and stern Sister Cecilia of the Colegio de Sta. Isabel, where I was a boarding student throughout high school. I remember being in a piano recital, and I've forgotten a passage, messed up and felt so embarrassed that I wanted to disappear. So I marvel and am so in awe at the skill and artistry that I witnessed from the young concert pianists presented on this tour, Marie-Laure Boulanger, Martin Surot, and Jean Dube.

This trip started out as a misadventure, with a two and a half hour weather delay in Atlanta which caused us to miss our Bilbao connection in Madrid-Barajas, which caused us to miss joining the rest of the group coming in from Charles de Gaulle in Paris , which caused us to miss the bus for the one-hour trip to San Sebastian. We had to find our own way in a taxi to the Bilbao bus depot, and then take a public bus to San Sebastian. We had five minutes to spare after purchasing our E8.65 bus ticket, but we finally made it to dinner with the group at our hotel. Voila!

Madrid-Barajas, by the way, has a spanking new terminal, a marble and steel work of art rising up from the semi-arid Barajas landscape with a roof undulating like a wave and grid supports fanning out of a center spine like fish bones. Inside was chaos. Long lines at the economy ticket counters and check-in stations, while the business class counters were empty and manned by several staff just standing around. Service was nowhere to be had. We could have made our flight connection if we were allowed priority check-in, but we were brusquely denied and sent back to the end of the line. The next flight would be four hours later.

But why are we in San Sebastian? It's to appreciate the Basque influence in Ravel's music, for his mother was Basque, and women who helped raise him sang to him Basque lullabies and folk songs, and these rhythms found expression in his Alborada del Gracioso and the opera "L'Heure Espagnole," "La Valse," "Rhapsodie," the famous "Bolero" , and the unfinished Basque Concerto, "Zazpiak Bat". I was only familiar with "Bolero", because of the movie "10" and Bo Derek, but that piece written in his later years was an embarrassment to Ravel. He considered it trivial, and wondered why "a piece for orchestra without music" could be so popular.

We're also in San Sebastian to understand Ravel as a man. He never married, he lived with his mother, and when she died it sent him into despair. He was a meticulous dandy, and his house in Montfort L'Amaury, Le Belvedere, just outside Paris, where he worked until his death, was filled with collections of first editions, Japanese prints, tiny mechanical toys, and many small beautiful, fragile objects like a woman's house. His sexual orientation is still a mystery, but there is no doubt about his place as a big figure in French music. He was quoted to say that a Basque is full of passion but only reveals it to a few intimates, countering critics who viewed him as aloof and reticent.

Our hotel in San Sebastian, atop Monte Igueldo, offered a spectacular view of the city and the beach and the Cantabrian coast. As you descend the funicular attached to our perch, the view is picturesque with houses built against the hills following the slope down into the sea, their windows spilling over with flowers, and the surrounding hills covered with lavender. The beach is dotted with cabanas, and holiday visitors spread out on the sand, with many women sunning with their bikini tops off. There's a mile-long promenade lined by bistros and cafes and benches for watching the world go by. Across the beach is the pedestrian shopping area, festive and with lots of people milling about the shops. We wandered into a Picasso exhibit of his bullfight watercolors, which I'd never seen before. When I visited the Picasso museum in Barcelona three years ago, the last trip I took with Johnny, I brought home prints of his erotica drawings. Here I marveled at how this master never failed to emphasize the bull's erectile parts in every frame!

On the bus to Ciboure, the French Basque of Ravel's birth, I learned the significance of the signs shown throughout these parts which proudly declare that 4+3=1.The Basque is fiercely independent, with a unique language and culture, and has been involved in separatist struggles for generations. There are the four Spanish Basque provinces of Alava, Guipuzcoa, Viscaya, and Navarre, and three French provinces of Basse-Navarre, Labourd, and Soule. These signs, which dot the highways, express the unity between the French and Spanish provinces and bring them together in the popular separatist movement.

We stopped in Bilbao to visit the Guggenheim Museum. It is a soaring, winged piece of art on the banks of the Nervion River smack in the center of the city and designed by the American Frank Gehry. It is magnificent, structurally complex, and its reputation well-deserved. The flower topiary puppy at its entrance gives a warm and homey welcome. Showing then was "RUSSIA!" an exhibition of art made in the USSR during the cold war. There was an art installation there showing through the mixed media of photos, video, sounds, 3-dimensional compositions and participatory viewing, how psychiatry was used to control and repress through electric shock treatments of dissidents. It was very disturbing for me, and destabilized my stance of maintaining an arm's length distance from the state hospital policies that I have to apply to the psychiatric patients I work with.

In Ciboure, we stayed in the neighboring beach resort of St. Jean-de-Luz, across the river Nivelle and along the coast south of Biarritz and Bayonne. Ciboure is holding the Raveliad festival, featuring winners of the Academie Ravel Music Competitions. The three nights of concerts we attended were held in the Église Saint Vincent, a 16th century church where Ravel was christened. Ciboure has a medieval background and its old World charm dates back to the 13th and 14th centuries, with historic relics all around the town. There was plenty of time during the day to explore and shop, lay out on the beach, and savor fresh seafood from the Basque coast.

We stayed for a night in Amboise after a seven hour drive from the coast through the reforested swamps of France and Bordeaux and the Loire Valley, stopping briefly on the way to visit the chateau and gardens of Villandry. Then we were in the storied and ancient Loire Valley, where we visited Chenonceaux to discover its significance for Debussy. Marie Laur Barcat, a history professor at the University of Tours, and an expert on Chenonceaux, didn't know how Chenonceaux was important to Debussy, but she was curious and agreed to research the subject. She couldn't wait to share everything that she'd unearthed with us. She was so passionate and inspiring, and this excitement was part of her work! I was thinking then how I disliked my work environment, and how I longed to feel energized and electrified by my work and to have people around who are eager and creative and inspiring. I questioned whether it was a reasonable trade off being a robot at work eight hours a day, five days a week, for two more years in exchange for Georgia state retirement benefits.

After visiting Chenonceaux, which spans the river Cher, we stopped briefly for liqueur tasting at the Fraise D'or, then Vochek, our Polish bus driver, took us through the streets of Paris to settle at our hotel near the Opera Garnier. The familiar sights went by:

the Eiffel Tower, Arc de Triomphe, Sacre Coeur, Place de la Concorde, Notre Dame and Isle de Cité, Champs Elysées, then we were on the left bank of the Seine, passing Pont Neuf, Musee D'Orsay, then Tullieres gardens, the Louvre, then the shops along St. Honore. We went down the Avenue D'opera, and checked in our hotel on Rue D'Antin. Dinner that night was a 5-course, wine-paired affair at Le Train Bleu, an elaborate belle epoque restaurant in Gare de Lyon.

On our second day in Paris we woke up to the BBC news of a foiled terroristic plot to board at Heathrow and blow up ten planes in the sky on their way to the US. We wondered how it would affect our return trip, but we went on with our program without a hitch. We've been in the countryside and the Basque coast, the Loire Valley and all of these seemed like an unreal world. Those places had picture-perfect villages, flower boxes on every cottage window, giant planter baskets with blooms hanging on town lampposts, and bucolic rural scenery of farms and trees and cows. They had brilliant sun and cool weather, and a homogenous people of one race, all smiling and contented. Now we're jolted by reality. Well, almost.

The big controversy in Paris then was over the proposed city ruling to ban topless sunbathing and thong bikinis during Paris Plage. On its third year, the event transforms the river banks of the Seine in Central Paris into a tropical beach with 2,000 tons of fine sand trucked in, then palm trees and beach chairs and umbrellas were laid out for sweltering Parisians to take in the sun as if they're in Palm Beach or Mallorca. I thought only Hollywood could dream up something like this. They had just dismantled this 2M Euro fantasy when we arrived, but I saw remnants of it as I jogged along the Seine every morning.

From Paris we visited Ravel's house in Montfort L'Amaury. There on Ravel's piano, our tour organizer from San Francisco, Bill Wellborn, and Parisian Marie-Laur Boulanger, gave a concert of Ravel music. The next day, we visited Debussy's house in Saint-Germain-en-Laye, where the noted French pianist Dominique Merlet gave a lecture on Debussy, dissecting and demonstrating the chords and scales he used in his compositions, and following with a recital of Ravel, Debussy and Liszt. A concert of the four hand piano by Ravel and Debussy followed, with Bill Wellborn and Marie-Laur playing alongside a newly married couple who played Debussy together with such rapport and finesse it could break your heart.

On our way to the Channel Islands, we listened to Walter Gieseking play "Claire de Lune" on a recording so ephemeral and exquisite it made you feel like you could caress the moonlight.

I didn't know Guernsey and Jersey were part of the Channel Islands. I thought one was a cow, and the other was what New Jersey was named after. We crossed the channel from the medieval town of St Malo, which at one point was controlled by pirates, and from its port Jacques Cartier sailed to discover Canada. On the ferry there was a group of happy girls, and one of them was wearing a makeshift tiara and a band across her chest saying "Bride to Be". They were in St. Malo for a bachelorette party, and she was getting married next Saturday in Jersey, where she and her fiancé lived. They were so cute I took their photo, and getting off the ferry later they squealed in glee to see me again and introduced themselves. The bride to be was Emma and her bridesmaid Sophie was her sister. Jersey was part of our tour because Debussy was a ladies' man, and he ran off to Jersey to tryst with his mistress Emma Bardac, whom he later married after she divorced her much older and richer husband, and after her affair with Faure. We're now in British territory, and English is spoken here, though the people claim an independence from Great Britain and circulate their own Jersey pound, which is not negotiable anywhere else.

It is a beautiful if rocky island resort. We had a private concert in the old church concert hall by Jean Dube, a Liszt piano competition winner. He was fantastic, a perfect finale for this musical tour which combined musical pleasures with history, gastronomy, oenology, culture, and a wonderful group of people. After a visit to Giverny to relax in Monet's garden, we checked into an old Manor in Rolleboise that overlooked the Seine just outside of Paris. There we got dressed up for our gala dinner and said goodbye. My return trip was uneventful, despite the terrorist alert. The only telling sign was the confiscation of my newly purchased Dior red lipstick, classified as a forbidden item.

CHAPTER 30: Amongst Giants, California the Beautiful

We had to get on a jet plane and fly four and a half hours from Atlanta to walk under the spell of these giants in the pristine snow-covered Giant Forest of Sierra Nevada, in the Sequoia National Park, in California. My friend Mary had a conference in Palm Springs, and we thought it would be fun to take a side trip and to snowshoe among the majestic sequoia redwoods. Well, what we thought was a two hour drive from Palm Springs wound up being over six hours. First of all, we left Palm Springs without a map. We thought we could just get on the road and follow signs to the giants, being that they grew nowhere else in the world. The random routes we picked, however, fortuitously gave us the full flavor of the California landscape. Outside of Palm Springs, I-10 offered the alien scenery of white wind turbines against blue skies and stark earth. The San Gorgonio Pass is a wind tunnel, and there are 3000 windmills looking like they are made from the same polymer material as the Star Wars storm troopers, with their three-prong blades reminiscent of the Mercedes-Benz logo. These erect wind catchers are planted in rows 700 feet apart like an orange grove as far as the edge of the San Jacinto mountains in the Coachella valley, looming on top of ridges like sentinels from outer space. We got on I-215, and briefly on I-15, traveling on the winding roads that cradle the San Bernardino Mountain with nothing to see but the road and the bare mountainside. We turned towards Route 395, which cuts across the Mojave Desert with its miles and miles of shimmering road reflecting the glitter of the sun. We admired the fortitude of the Joshua trees surviving in that harsh climate. Then, approaching Bakersfield on Route 58, we first passed Edwards AFB then it's suddenly green and fertile with orange groves heavy with ripe fruit ready for picking. Many had fallen from the branch and laid rotting on the ground. There are rows of grape vines trained to grow formally on trellises, pastures of grazing cows, and cookie-cutter housing developments built in the middle of nowhere.

Then we were in Tulare County, in the Sierra Nevada foothills, and it was dark. The climb to the Giant Forest was a mere twenty-three miles from the foothills, but we didn't know it was a tightly wound road embracing the mountain with tight hairpin turns and convoluted spiral ascents that required intense focus and prayer, especially in the darkness and there was nothing else on the road but the prospect of a wandering hungry bear. It was unnerving to find out later that this road, Route 198, is carved overlooking deep ravines with snow embankments as high as seven feet on its mountain side. It took us two and a half hours to reach Wuksachi Lodge, which sits at 6,500 feet, only to find out that the restaurant stopped serving meals five minutes before our arrival. The lodge had no room service, and the nearest food joint was in the foothills, which we left behind two and a half hours ago. But these were nice people and they called the kitchen, and they were only too happy to take our orders from their regular menu, and they allowed us to stay until dessert. We forgave the restaurant its shortcoming in fulfilling its advertised claim of specializing in gourmet Sierra alpine cuisine. The snow covered forest outside our lodge window, the crisp 41F degree sunny weather and blue skies, the cedar scented air, and the friendly and charming lodge staff made up for the bland and limp pan seared red mountain trout, the unrecognizable meat loaf, the pasta special with Italian sausage and kalamata olives which I had to complain about because there were only traces of olives and two thin slices of sausage in the dish. Perhaps the restaurant is up to its advertised standards during their regular season, which starts May 15. We booked for early April, which was at the end of the winter season and the resort activities shop had closed. There were no more rentals available for snowshoes, cross country skis, or snow boots. The Crystal Cave with marble stalactites and stalagmites was closed, and the road to Kings Canyon was off limits.

We could hike in the snow, however, so we set out with excitement to see the big trees and headed to the Giant Forest Museum for information. We took pictures of the General Sherman Tree, the largest and oldest living thing at 52,508 cubic feet and over 2,000 years old. Wow! We asked directions to the Giant Forest trail, and set out on our own to be with the big trees. We underestimated the challenges of hiking on deep snow, softened by the 41F degree weather and we didn't know that the trails were marked with symbols on trees and that the trails were not alike. We were following a trails map to a grove of big trees on the Congress trail, but we lost our direction. We followed footprints on the snow that were going up higher and higher and which led us to a slippery narrow ledge against the mountain over 200 feet of steep ravine. There were footprints here, so we figured it had to lead somewhere, and so we continued, being careful to plant our boots so we wouldn't slip.

After rounding the side of the mountain we lost the trail signs and the footprints disappeared. We clambered over fallen trees hoping to pick up the trail but we fell thigh deep into the softened snow and suddenly it dawned on us that we could fall into even deeper snow over god-knows-what. The fog was starting to come in, and it was getting darker. I conceded to Mary's judgment that we should retrace our steps and return instead of continuing on trying to pick up the Congress trail from the Alta trail. When we emerged after four hours in the forest we realized that the Alta trail is an advanced trail, and we really had no business being there. From here on Mary didn't trust me, and her decisions prevailed, leading us on safe, sedate walks. In a way I was glad we got lost on that first day. After all, all's well that ends well.

Like everyone else, we climbed the Moro Rock. It is 400 steps and half a mile to the top of this granite monolith, and we were lucky to find it free of snow even at its peak elevation of 6,725 feet. From there, we viewed the vista of the Sierra Nevada range, the Giant Forest, the Kaweah River, the Kern Canyon, and the great Western Divide. We drank in the whole breathtaking magnitude of it all. Mt. Whitney, the highest point in the US at 14,491 feet, crowns the Sierra. My brother Mike and sister-in-law Pilar, came from Fresno to join us on this climb, and they spent the day hiking with us. They invited us to see the wonders of Yosemite, and he planned to return to Sequoia and Kings Canyon to camp in the summer.

After four days of natural wonder we were ready for the man-made wonders of Palm Springs. We took the quick route back on I-99 and I-5, which sadly eliminated our view of the amazing and various landscapes. Approaching Palm Springs from I-10, we made our way to the Westin Resort in Rancho Mirage. On one side of the road here are gated luxury housing developments with multimillion dollar price tags, imported shrubs and trees and grasses, and man-made lakes serving as hazards in verdant signature golf courses, of which there are over 150, and which soak up thousands of gallons of water in the maintenance of their lush greens. But not to worry. The Coachella Valley lies on top of an aquifer that bubbles with hot springs and cool waters filtered from the melting alpine peaks of surrounding mountains. The Colorado River feeds a concrete aqueduct that irrigates the desert fields for produce worth over $500 million annually.

On the other side is Indian land. With only the road separating it from the lush settlement on one side, we saw the authentic arid Sonoran desert landscape, with its unrelenting sun, tumbleweeds, mesquite shrubs, and the multi-purpose creosote. We learned that the Cahuilla Indians of the region are the richest today because of three smart women who went to Washington DC during the homesteading era and did the paperwork for a deal that gave them 40% ownership of the desert when the railroad came calling. They lease the lands, own banks, businesses, and the casinos. The biggest of these, the Agua Caliente Casino Resort and Spa, is currently undergoing a $300 million expansion.

I couldn't wait to visit the San Andreas Fault, the cosmic point where two tectonic plates, the Pacific and the North American, slip and slide about 35 millimeters a year in opposite directions, creating tremors in the earth or great earthquakes that can decimate Palm Springs and the rest of Southern California. The earthquakes here rearrange mountains and lakes and coastlines, and push California towards Canada. I had imagined a deep, dark chasm running to the core of the earth, but instead the rupture is a ribbon of tropical oases encircling the bottom of the San Jacinto Mountains, rife with gurgling streams, palm trees, and many birds and creatures such as rattlesnakes and tourists.

For a different kind of adventure, we took the Palm Springs Aerial Tram, the largest rotating tram car in the world. It is an engineering marvel, constructed in the rugged Chino Canyon with the use of helicopters, and it offers a literally breathtaking ride to the summit of the San Jacinto Mountain, bringing us to 10,804 feet in 10 minutes and offering a spectacular 360 degree view of the entire Coachella Valley. For the rest of our visit we did our usual thing, playing golf, trying Valley cuisine, attending corporate parties, and so on. On the last day of Mary's conference the corporate closing event was at the Empire Polo Grounds, one of sixteen in the area, each with a grassy expanse the size of nine football fields. We dressed up to attend an abbreviated polo match complete with an enthusiastic fast-talking announcer. We got to meet the horses and their riders, then dined under Arabian-style tents with live music and moonlight, pretending Prince Charles was in attendance and we were ladies of the court . A perfect fantasy in a town where streets are named after Hollywood stars and electricity bills run sky high to cool fancy homes built in the hottest and driest place in the USA. That's desert living.

On the flight back to Atlanta we were flying low in Skywest's 76-seater CRJ 100 to Salt Lake, and we looked down to a panoramic and mesmerizing aerial view of the golden sands of the Sonora and the Algodones Dunes. I'd never realized before that California was so beautiful!

Chapter 31: YaYa's In The Coolest Neighborhood of NY City

November 6-10, 2014

It seemed like a good idea. First it was Anicia's and my annual NYC trip, using my Delta companion promotional coupon. Kathy got a whiff of our plans and wanted to come along. As I booked a 3-BR apartment in Bushwick, it was perfect. We had an early flight to get in as many hours in NYC as we could. We persuaded our landlord to have us check in early to the consternation of the cleaning lady who in her haste to get the apartment ready forgot to replenish the toilet paper. We had to forage for facial tissue in our pocketbooks and made do until we could get to a store and purchase a roll. No big deal, we were refreshed and embarked on a walk to Roberta's, the pizza house to go to when in Brooklyn. None of us were any good in navigating from a map so we stopped at a corner convenience store for directions and was told it was a long walk. Not a problem, we had a taxi service number to call and in five minutes we were picked up at the corner of Central and Myrtle and dropped off at Roberta's in a flash. It is a five minute wait for Brooklyn taxis to come to your door on weekdays and six minutes on weekends. Roberta's, if you didn't know that it was the coolest pizza house in Brooklyn, you would not dare venture in. It is a graffiti encased hole in the wall derelict-looking place, but once you're past the red door, you come into an inviting space warmed by the wood-fired oven wafting aromas of basil, olive oil, and every delicious smell to tempt your taste. Manuel, our second generation Filipino waiter recently transplanted from San Francisco made us immediately welcomed and suggested a citrusy light ale to accompany our order of Bee Sting pizza, their signature spicy concoction of tomato sauce, cheese, guanciale, basil, and the surprise ingredient, honey! Immediately it was our favorite. We also loved the mussels marinara with cheese and dredges of smoked pork to flavor the soup. The broth was so divine we had to ask for spoons to collect the last drops. After our lunch, we came out of the red door to a light drizzle but we had umbrellas and warm coats so we checked the neighborhood and found an organic market with persimmons and chia seeds with very good prices. Stocking up on cheese and salume, Starbucks coffee and Utz crab chip, we found a wine shop to complete our comfort food supply for the next five days in Bushwick.

We felt we were hip strolling in the seventh coolest neighborhood in the world, as proclaimed by Diana Vreeland in Vogue's September issue. Next door to Roberta's, its sister restaurant Blanca, double Michelin-starred, where the 25-course chef menu costs $700 per couple, is visited by the rich and famous, and reservations to its twelve tables open up only every thirty days. There are affordable other cool places to be seen though. Michael, Anicia's local son took us to order dirty martinis at his favorite speakeasy, Featherweight, which unfortunately to my classic-dry martini accustomed palate, tasted like salad dressing, which I couldn't imbibe, uncool as I may be. Later we filled up on food that sticks to the bone at Eastwick.

Continuing our pursuit of cool places we explored Eataly, an Italian gourmet food center on 23rd and 5th, marqueed by Mario Batali, and we fell in love. We compared the Plaza Food Court and Todd English Food Hall, and we thought Eataly wins the charm, the vibe, the cool factor. The place has warmth and the bustle of a market, the food offerings are elemental and authentic. You can see fresh fish with glistening eyes and with healthy smell, vegetables that are fresh picked before it is cooked simply and purely, pasta looks chewy as it comes off the cutter gadget, and breads with crusts that crackles and fresh from the oven. Anicia and Kathy shared a whole seared flounder, while I had the bacalao and grilled polpo small plates, both we gave thumbs up. You can buy from the market all ingredients that are necessary to duplicate what you ate at the restaurants. There is an Eataly in Chicago and a third one coming up in Southern California.

Crossing Williamsburg Bridge to Manhattan after figuring out the subway lines, we watched Ewan McGregor, Maggie Gyllenhaal, and Cynthia Nixon perform in Tom Stoppard's "The Real Thing", which we gave a thumbs down, the play, for being outdated, but we loved the actors. We shivered in the cold, trying to flag down a yellow cab as hundred others, after seeing the farcical and utterly hilarious "The Gentlemen's Guide to Love and Murder", last year's Tony winner for Best Musical. We thought we got lucky to be offered a ride by an unmarked taxi, and fortunately, we had the prescience to ask for the tariff before jumping in from the wintry wind because the price was $80 from the regular $30. Two more approached us at $130 and $80 each. Yellow cabs cruised by, and we flagged them all but subsequently learned that lighted roof mounted taxi numbers signaled availability. We got lucky when a taxi discharged a passenger at our feet and we got in before anyone else grabbed it from under our noses. At the MET opera in Lincoln Center, we missed the first act of Mozart's "Die Zauberflote", having arrived at 2 pm for the one o'clock matinee. We proclaimed ourselves growing in wisdom by treating these senior moments as adventures rather than disasters. Anyway, we were having a great time during Act 1 enjoying lunch and the view of Central Park and Columbus Circle from the Center Cafe Bar at Time Warner Center.

We shopped for a hat on 57th Ave after Anicia left hers in a taxi, and I got offers for my boiled wool hand-crafted hat from Latvia and my fashion cred was affirmed by compliments on the train, and admiring notice from the street, for my Italian snake skin Donald Pliner cowboy boots. We felt as fashionable as Carrie and friends in the City, alas without the Sex.

Our serious shopping was reserved for Chinatown, starting on Canal St. and winding through the alleys of Mulberry, Broome, then to Mott St. We googled what's trending in fashion and picked bargains in plaids, wine colors and cobalt blue, and fake furs. After establishing trustworthiness with a store owner who has a Filipino employee, we were approved to view her shipment of high quality fake designer bags and were led through dark narrow hallways to a padlocked back room filled with Louis Vuittons, Chanels, Diors, etc. Bargaining for the best price for these knock-offs delayed our rendezvous with my brother Banong and Loretta at Hop Kee, our to-go-to restaurant since our US arrival in 1967. As we were arriving, I encountered Madeline, my daughter JayJay's childhood friend from Atlanta, as she was leaving. She too was making a point of eating at Hop Kee whenever in NYC and ordering the snails to keep the tradition began since she was a little girl, and she came to the city with our family and we booked rooms at the Plaza, to see the store holiday window displays. What a small world, and a serendipitous meeting.

My YaYas from Atlanta were game to have the snails. After our big Chinese lunch, it needed an Italian gelato for a proper finish so we walked to Little Italy by way of Grand St. to pick up some fruits for breakfast and to accompany our cheese snack. We discovered the nutritional value and anti-oxidant properties of persimmons and pomegranates and are now devotees of these ancient and exotic fruits.

Our culinary adventure was capped by dinner on our last night at Public, a Michelin-starred Asian fusion restaurant in Nolita, where the manager is Alex, who the YaYas met from a previous trip when he managed West, in the Upper Westside two years ago. He is the son of a friend, and he gave us the VIP treatment with complimentary cava rose and mushroom ceviche appetizer.

Our return flight was at 8 pm, and after a reprise of Bee Sting at Roberta's for lunch we decided to take an earlier flight. When we arrived at Hartsfield-Jackson shortly after 6 pm instead of 11 pm we decided to play a prank on Linda C. We called and told her that we changed to an earlier flight and we could make it to her dinner party after all. As she apparently cancelled the invitation since none could make it, she had no dinner prepared, but she didn't hesitate to have us come over anyway and she'd put together something. We called off our prank of course, but it was lovely to know we won't go hungry with friends like her.

"There are no foreign lands. It is the traveler only who is foreign." – Robert Louis Stevenson

CHAPTER 32: Why Go to Cuba?

Havana, Cienfuegos, Trinidad, Sancti Spiritu, Santa Clara, Pinar del Rio

January 29- February 5, 2012

Havana in low light, especially at dawn, beguiles like a beautiful apparition, with her silhouette framed by a pink and orange sky and her face reflected in the shimmer of the breaking surf of the Malecon. But alas, the sun rises, and she's exposed in broad daylight. Her bones are broken, her sinews anemic, her skin is peeling and scarred with deep cuts and discolored blemishes, and her body is draped in the plebeian fashion of the hoi polloi. She tries hard to please. Some parts of her have been restored and there you can imagine that she was once elegant and beautiful. She moved with the infectious rhythms of the rumba and bolero. She was desired by the mighty and the powerful and the unscrupulous. Yes, she had an ignominious past, and it still informs her behavior today.

On my second day I was relaxing with a drink at the hotel lounge and tapping my feet to a rumba and this young man asked me to dance. Soon he was hustling me, said he was twenty six years old and asked how old I was. So I told him I was thirty six years old (hah, I was sixty-nine) and he nodded his approval, and intensified his lobbying for my company. These jineteros and jineteras are everywhere. They offer to take you in their taxi, to the best restaurants, to the shows, to your hotel bed and to have sex with you. But there's no prostitution in Cuba, that's the official line. If you hit it off, they'll ask you to buy them presents, tell you their grandmother or child is sick and ask you for money, and then if you have lots of money, they'll marry you.

Life in Cuba, as they say, es no facil. The minimum wage is around $20/month, and though they get food ration coupons, it's not enough and they have to buy other necessities from the CUC (Convertible Cuban Peso) stores. 1 CUC is $0.87. The local peso is worthless (1 Peso=$0. 24) and Cubans only use it to pay their water and electric bills. The black market thrives, but can only serve you if you have CUC currency. Goods are smuggled from Ecuador, Haiti, Venezuela and the Dominican Republic. There are spies to report these illegal activities, but life is hard for everyone, so this is not enforced rigorously if the right favors are exchanged. In the past three months, there were monumental changes. Where Cubans could not buy and sell property in the past, now they have the limited ability to do so. They can own, for example, up to two houses, one in the city and the other on the coast or the mountain. They can also now borrow money from the bank. How Cubans with $20 monthly wages can do this is mind boggling, but there's money coming from somewhere. Obama had eased money remittances to relatives in Cuba and also opened unlimited travel for US relatives. As limited family entrepreneurship is now allowed, mostly to serve the tourist industry, Paladares (restaurants) and Casa Particulares (B&B) are opening up. At first they were extremely regulated, because they were not to compete with government run establishments. They were limited in the number of tables and foods they could provide and could only employ family members. But even if it's a snail's pace for the rest of us, things are changing at a dizzying speed in Cuba.

Tourism is now a major industry since the Soviet collapse in the early 90's that threw Cuba into economic hardship. The revolution had to keep its paternalistic promises and was forced to adopt capitalistic practices to feed the people. Tips are expected everywhere, and you quickly get the impression that the economy runs on tips. You can't use the toilets without dropping your spare change in the collection plate, or you won't have toilet paper and soap, and you must straddle it, because they are without seats or lids. As much as excellent universal health care is touted, water is unsafe unless boiled, so you must buy bottled water. Food safety can be suspect, as six of us went down with GI upsets, including me, and one had required IV infusion. One soon becomes wary of people's friendliness, as a tip is expected for every small helpful gesture. I was chatting with a young mother admiring her two small children, and she wasted no time in asking me for my hotel toiletries after I check out. I was asked to pony up 5 CUC (!) to get my photo in a vintage car. Disembarking from the steam train in the touristy former sugar plantation of Iznaca, we were overwhelmed by swarms of women importuning us for soaps, lotions, and other gifts. Tourists who don't understand poverty are guilty of shaping this behavior, they make beggars of poor people.

As much as I fell in love with the dashing rebel Che Guevarra, and even Fidel in his own way, their revolution had gone on for too long, and though it might be hard for Cuba to have an Arab spring, as they are very limited in their cyber connectedness, it won't be long before an upheaval takes place. The revolution ironically made education a priority benefit for the people, and now these educated young men and women are looking to test their wings in the big world, and Cuba is too small and narrow now. There are underground bloggers planting roots and spreading their message in cyberspace. They are finding a way, despite crackdowns and being roughed up by government goons. What do you do with doctors and lawyers, multi-linguists, historians and artists and engineers forced to work in tourism as guides, bartenders, waiters, as it is the sector where one can earn serious money through tips? Soon they will get ideas and will want to test them. Just you wait.

It's dusk and the gentle breeze is soothing, the musicians (for tips) are playing a bolero. I'll light up my Cohiba and sip and savor my 15-year old Santiago in the gardens of my legendary hotel overlooking the crashing surf and the Malecon, now filling up with Cubans strolling after a day of labor in perhaps a dead end occupation. Would I return? Nah!

CHAPTER 33: Dubai, Abu Dhabi

I felt like I was in the Philippines as soon as I landed at Dubai International Airport. I got there after a fourteen hour flight from Washington Dulles and a one and a half hour connecting flight from Atlanta. It's eight hours ahead, so I arrived in the mid-afternoon of the following day. The staff greeting arrivals and directing them to the Passport Control Area are all Filipinos. The 2,000 plus passengers simultaneously deplaning from Qatar, Bagram, Bahrain, Muscat, Riyadh, Oman, Kuwait, Doha, Amman, Addis Ababa, Hyderabad, Kish Island, Cairo, Karachi, Mumbai, Jeddah, Singapore, Bangkok, Prague, and Washington DC, were processed in forty double-staffed stations by kandura-clad Emiratis, who were unhurried and unsmiling in their tasks. U.S. citizens are automatically given thirty-day tourist visas on arrival, without paperwork or fees. I was en-route with my tour group to our hotel in less than two hours. Arriving at Royal Ascot Hotel, I was checked in and shown to my room by Filipino staff. As we were on our own until the start of our guided tour the following day I decided to check the place without delay and took the Metro to Dubai Mall. The Dubai Metro, operational since 2009, which at 75 km holds the Guinness record of the longest driverless rail system in the world, is a sleek and efficient transport system that takes you to the important tourist destinations. It has two lines currently, with plans to expand into three more. The forty-five platform-edged, air-conditioned stations are housed in ultra-contemporary oyster shaped gold structures. It has two fares, the regular and Gold class, costing from 2 AED to 28 AED ($0.54-$7.60) based on zones traveled, plus approximately one-third more for Gold class, which has more room and is uncrowded. The interior is luxurious with airplane-like seats done in a calming sea palette of royal blue, turquoise, and blue-grays. There is a separate coach for women and children. There are uniformed attendants, mostly Filipinos, who travel up and down to make sure you are using the appropriate compartment.

Dubai Mall boasts as the world's largest mall with 1,200 stores, cinemas, restaurants, play areas, an ice rink which can host hockey games and many more. It has a Bloomingdale's, Galleries Lafayette, PF Chang's, California Pizza, Starbucks, and every other US, European and British establishment. The sales staff are mostly Filipinos. In the Mall of the Emirates, which looks like Milan's Galleria Vittorio Emanuele, only bigger, there is a snow park and ski run. In the Madinat Jumeriah, billed as an Arabian Resort, and which has a lagoon and gondolas like in Venice, there are opulent souks that sell mainly goods from India, China and Egypt. In the man-made Dubai Marina, architectural wonders and breathtaking skyscrapers vie for world records. In the man-made Palm Island, so called because of its shape, the opulent Atlantis Resort sits at the apex, and is the duplicate of the original in the Bahamas. The palm's side branches are dotted with million dollar villas that can be purchased by foreigners, except for the land, which is leased for ninety-nine years. The Burj Khalifa, with one hundred sixty-four floors, looks down at New York City's Empire State which is a mere 53% of its size. The Burj Al Arab, the only seven-star hotel in the world, is very exclusive, with rooms ranging from $2000-$25,000 per night, the latter comes with a butler and 24-carat plumbing. If you can't stay for the night the only other way to gain a peek of the hotel is to book a reservation in one of their fine restaurants. I had friends who took me to dinner at Al Mahara, their signature restaurant. The dinner tab was a month's mortgage payment. The food was fine, but I had similar fare in Atlanta's Bacchanalia and Eugene's for one tenth of the cost.

Why do people pay these absurd prices in Dubai? To spend like a Sheik is an irresistible come-on that speaks to every man's vanity, and is a stroke of marketing genius.

Dubai and Abu Dhabi are once again on a roll with their construction and development, after a brief pause during the world financial crisis which saw Dubai overstretched and needed a bail-out from neighboring oil-rich Abu Dhabi. Abu Dhabi, following Dubai's example, is developing Saadiyat Island into a luxury resort and cultural district, which will hold the Louvre and Guggenheim Museums, the National Museum and Performing Arts Center.

The Bedouin lifestyle is no longer visible here. The only remaining symbol of cultural identity with which you can differentiate Emiratis, the UAE native born, from expatriates is in the wardrobe. The men wear the elegant white kandura, teamed with the checked head cover keffiyeh and held in place by the cord agal. Their women are shrouded in black abayas, with hijab or niqab for head and face covers, or the hide-all black burqa.

There is hardly any opportunity to interact with an Emirati. They comprise a mere twelve percent of the population, and the rest of the eight million are expatriates, mainly laborers, service workers, experts, professionals, business partners, and consultants from India, Pakistan, Egypt, Russia, the Philippines, and from Great Britain, the U.S. and Europe.

The U.A.E., formed by a federation of seven kingdoms and independent since 1971, started as a group of feuding nomadic tribes and incredibly transformed itself into this modern megapolis in a matter of a generation. Sheikh Zayed bin Sultan Al Nahyan, the founder of United Arab Emirates, was raised as a desert Bedouin, scarcely had any education beyond the basics of Islam, but with a clear vision and wisdom, guided the development of his country to benefit all citizens, using the wealth created by the discovery of oil. He built roads, bridges, hospitals, schools, housing and distributed land to all citizens. The Bedouins, still familiar with the harsh existence of living in the desert had held him in great affection and he ruled until his death in 2004 at age eighty-six. Compared to other Arabian gulf countries he promoted a more liberal social and political policies and tolerance for other religions and cultures. These polices however have not kept pace with the dizzying economic and infrastructure and visual transformation of the U.A.E.

The U.A.E. is dependent on labor and technical expertise from the expatriates who comprise 88.5% of the population. They have no stake in the country and remain as guest workers. If they lose their jobs they are deported. Children of expatriates born in the U.A.E. may be deported unless they are in school or have a job. Though there are no taxes, expatriates are not eligible for social security, free education for their children, or health care. There is no pathway to citizenship, except on the rare occasion of an Emirati man marrying a non-Emirati woman, then their children are citizens but not vice versa.

A man may have up to four wives if he can afford it but women can have only one husband. With increased female education and participation in the labor pool, women are marrying later, or choosing not to marry Emirati men, and certainly fewer are giving consent to multiple marriages. The ruling body encourages large families. In Aijam, a 63-year old Emirati with 92 children, is on the news, about to take his eighteenth wife, a young woman from Pakistan. One of his wives was a Filipina. He promised the Sheik 100 children, and the Sheik in return takes on the financial burden of raising them. Many still follow traditional patterns and marry their cousins. Congenital diseases have a high incidence, particularly, hemoglobinopathies, autism, and Down's syndrome. There is inadequate service for the disabled, due to lack of expertise and education. The disabled are kept at home and families are left to deal with it. There is no election and the legislature is only advisory and appointed by the ruling class. There is increasing discrepancy in economic status, as the business and financial sector is dominated by the powerful merchant families and the royal family and contracts are awarded based on personal relationships. The ordinary Emirati prefers to work for the government and has avoided the more competitive private sector, prompting the ruling body to institute Emeratisation policies, which required foreign companies to have hiring quotas for Emeratis. However, this is a thorny situation as Emeratis do not have the needed expertise and do not possess the work ethic needed in a competitive workplace.

The expatriates live in a parallel universe of their national affiliations, separate from other foreign nationals and the Emiratis. For those in the lower salary rungs, there may be exploitation and physical abuse. There is no sense of community between groups, and as one can be deported easily after one's employment ends, even after decades of toil building the nation, there is no civic engagement. It is incomprehensible, but for many who came from poor developing countries, working in the UAE permits one's family to survive.

I was jolted to attention by the dress code notice posted at the mall entrance; no shorts or skirts above the knees, no figure-hugging or cleavage-exposing attire, and shoulders should be covered. In the mosques, the dress code is more stringent, covered up to the wrists and ankles, and the head and neck under a veil or scarf. It's ironic, as the fashions displayed in the malls violate these rules. Despite the ultra modernity of its infrastructure and skyscrapers, and the abundance of material goods and luxury items and entertainment in the malls, and the appearance of Westernization, don't be fooled. There is no pork in the menu, alcohol is only available in hotel restaurants and bars and is expensive. You are awakened by the prayer call at dawn and at sunrise, and you'll hear the call again, wherever you are, at noon. In the gloaming, and at night when the last prayer call is heard, it is hypnotic and calming, a pristine moment for reflection. The weekend is Friday and Saturday, and the work week begins on Sunday.

So, on the surface the UAE looks like any developed Western country in its display of material and consumer wealth, but at the end of the day it is still a Muslim country ruled by Sharia law and is an autocratic state.

CHAPTER 34: Incredible India

March 2014

Delhi Jaipur Pushkar Agra Orccha Khajuraho Varanasi Sarnath Kolkata Mumbai

Visiting India was near the bottom of my travel destination, but my dream to see the world would not be complete without setting foot on this subcontinent where one-third of the human race lives. All I knew about India concerned Mahatma Gandhi, Mother Theresa, the Nehru jacket, its jewel-bedecked dark-eyed women wearing elegant and exquisite silk saris and who encrusted their foreheads with a ruby, and the celluloid portrayal of the lavish Maharajah lifestyle of the British during its two centuries of colonial rule. And yeah, the blockbuster "Slum-dog Millionaire". I had many Indian colleagues in my medical profession but I did not have any Indian personal friends. My aversion was shaped during my internship, and further cemented into prejudice from conflicted encounters with various forms of one-upmanship. Looking back, my experiences were with Indian men in the context of a very competitive professional milieu. I thought it was time to open my eyes, maybe I was missing something.

I arrived in Delhi on a Sunday. The city greeted me with a cacophony of car horns blaring, motor and pedal rickshaws careening with bells tinkling, street vendors screaming beyond the din, masses rushing to pick bargains, touts urging a sale at the best price. The smell of gasoline, dust, garbage, and animal excrement started a nauseous wave but then coriander, cumin, and samosas from the curbside food stalls quickly calmed the avalanche. The chaotic scene was contradicted by the brilliance of jewel-colored saris on the women and the bustling setting that was so purposeful, so full of life!

Deja vu. The road trip to Jaipur was a symphony of contrapuntal tunes of trumpeting vehicles, urging speed in a grid-locked highway ridden with diversions and potholes and stalled by cows, dogs and goats, lumbering along with motor traffic. The detour road was narrowed by makeshift truck stops and rest areas in shanty villages that catered to the needs of drivers who slept and rested during the day and drove at night. The major highway under construction since 2009 did not show any signs of completion anytime soon, but was getting its five minutes of fame with the upcoming national elections. In the rural villages scattered along the way, women in bright saris harvested the jatropha and rapeseed mustard fields, and the men eked a living from scraps. They lived in unfinished dwellings that were being built as funds became available, and where town halls failed to provide services, so that thrash were everywhere and men relieved themselves by merely turning their backs to the road. In wealthy Haryana, just outside Delhi, gleaming mirror and steel office skyscrapers and posh gated residential developments with names like Princess Park, Nirvana and Park Grandeura have sprouted like mushrooms to house the skilled workers in booming industries erected in planned industrial parks. In these gated enclaves, the rapidly growing middle class protects its fragile status. There are new millionaires and moneyed developers. They influence the dynastic political rulers. Nobody represents the poor but the poor overwhelms.

I had barely walked three blocks on the street where the legend of the Taj Mahal lives, when I was forced to turn and take refuge in the sanctuary of my hotel. In that brief excursion on my own I was accosted by hordes of grimy children begging for food or a few rupees or offering touts of snow globes of the Taj Mahal at the best price. When I withheld eye contact to ignore their supplication, I was taunted by chants of their imagined Chinese tongue and by their laughter, but then they left me alone. I was still shaking my head in mild disbelief, when I was jolted to attention by the screech of rubber meeting gravel and cement and then I felt a burning gash on my left ankle. A rickshaw just missed running over me but still made a side swept contact, inflicting a slight bruise on my ankle. I was crossing the street and was looking in the wrong direction, as India drives on the left the way the British do. I had barely collected myself when I had to give way to a herd of water buffaloes on their way to their spa in the River Yamuna, on which banks the city of Agra was built.

From then on, I watched where I stepped to avoid the piles of trash that collected everywhere, and the varied deposits of animal excrement lining my path. Cows lumbered along impassively and crossed the street with impunity, confident that humans would give way. I was told that there were hardly any cows hit by a vehicle or rickshaw. Rickshaws, the ubiquitous motorized tricycles, crowd the street and criss-cross out of lane without rhyme or reason. A juvenile goat herder was chasing and waving a stick at two run-away charges. And there were donkeys and dogs and a prancing white horse decorated to the hilt with gold tassels and bells on its way to a wedding. A tusked boar was foraging in a garbage pile. Engaged in the same task was an old man in faded red turban and matted grey-white beard grown down to where his clavicles joined at his throat. A woman in bright jewel-toned sari threw her leftover vegetarian meal to a cow.

All over, vendors displayed their goods, from toys to vegetables and flowers, on makeshift stalls that robbed the street of precious space. The air held the scents of the agora and reached one's nose depending on how the wind blew. One moment you held your breath as the smell of cow dung wafted by and the next breath you took might be full of the delicious aroma of cinnamon, cumin or cardamon, or the sweet perfume of roses and lilies. But you couldn't linger in reverie, as there was always someone insisting on your attention, to purchase something you already declined or ignored. I was looking for a square tablecloth, and the vendor persisted on showing me rectangles. And I felt threatened by the invasion of my physical space. Vendors thrust their wares at my face and followed me closely and sustained their offers longer than what was comfortable.

On the Bhopal Shtabdi express train from Agra on my way to Jhansi, I engaged a baggage handler. By the time I boarded the train two persons were handling my luggage. I gave the main guy his tip, indicating that the two should share it, but the other guy won't have it. I could argue and I know how to have my way but I was getting weary at this point of this tipping and I let it go. I felt like an ATM machine. The tourist was treated like a cash cow. I was told while shopping, "You are rich, you can pay this price." It seemed a tip was expected every time anybody did anything for you, requested or not. The doorman at a restaurant greeted me with a flower. He wanted a tip. Public toilets didn't provide soap and tissues. You had to tip the nice lady in sari with her toddler who handed those to you. I was at a monument site and a guy standing next to me started to tell me about the edifice, he expected a tip for his unsolicited commentary. This was all in addition to the bellhops and waiters and tour guides and drivers, and tour office representatives. I was beginning to feel abused. But reading the daily papers, I realized this is a way of life. Everybody is treated this way, not just the tourist. To get any service done, you must tip.

Here, the practice is institutionalized, it is part of the culture. To get a sought after government job, you must give the right staff a tip; to submit an application, to get an interview, and a bigger tip to land the job. Once you land the job, you may have to continue tipping in order to keep it. A Public Works Department timekeeper amassed millions this way, just on tips. Same goes for any business you want to conduct with any official agency. To get the building inspector to approve your plans to build, you must tip. To get the police to file a report of crime that was committed against you, you must tip. Trucks must tip the highway patrols so they can drive through. Then when you want the rules or law to be bent in your direction, you must tip. A guy cut off the finger of a police officer who was about to give him a violation ticket, which ordinarily could be forgiven with a tip. To make the government work for you, you must tip. A farmer drank poison when the farm bureau officer delayed inordinately to survey his loss for hailstorm damage to his tomato crop, because he failed to tip. And unable to tip, a vigilante women's gang has formed to get the officials in their rural village to file reports of domestic violence and rape, and to turn on electricity. The big politician does this, the littlest guy does this. A candidate for public office inserts cash in the newspapers delivered to a voter, a tip.

Everyone is a perpetrator, and everyone is a victim in this pecking order. A bridge over the Chambal River that had been approved for construction twenty-four years ago remains on the drawing board. This would alleviate transportation for rural villagers in three states, but the Public Works Department and Ministries of Environment have not found the time to complete their clearance. Perhaps the right tip has not been offered yet? The courts are busy ordering government agencies to do their mandates. I wonder if judges accept tips also.

The country has a very ancient and rich heritage, but it is a very young democracy. Tourism, too, is still very young, just a little over two decades in development. One could understand how everyone would try to make money off the tourist. Tips are a quick source of cash. The rural poor economy had changed with agrarian reform. It supplanted subsistence farming with cash crop planting. Many small farms succumbed to speculative real estate development and industrialization. The caste system, though abolished legally, still controls village mores. Reforms are disruptive of this society, and change is blocked that will threaten its way of life. In rural areas children are needed to help in the farm so they are not sent to school. Parents are enticed by free breakfast and lunch for the children, reducing their burden of feeding them. And girls especially are encouraged by the promise of a personal bike.

In urban areas, children are trained to beg, and often are main earners. Everyone on the street that the tourist encounters is just trying to make a living, the best way they can. The sheer numbers of the poor make getting the basic necessities very competitive. So it's part of the M.O. to flatter, to be servile, to undercut, trick, or manipulate. It's about gamesmanship. Why, CEO's and governments do it all the time. On the street everyone watches out for himself, man, cows, buffaloes, goats, rickshaws, cars. Anything goes, so it's up to everyone to know. The street is where life is lived and everyone is street-wise. Live and let live. Respect all living things.

And so life goes on, and nobody minds. The street markets are bustling, colorful, so alive, and weddings are celebrated in grand style, as vibrant and merry and full of hope as ever.

In one wedding on the street in Rajasthan there are pretty young ladies dancing to a live band, in brilliant saris of emerald, ruby, sapphire, gold, and amethyst. They followed newly-weds riding on decorated white horses. In another wedding, the couple was seated in a silver horse-drawn chariot, and one at night had huge column lights illuminating the gathering. Arranged marriages are still the norm. Though there are reports of bride kidnapping and abuse of women, the society is very protective and nurturing of women. They are respected as the guardian of the home and manager of the husband's income. The husband provides and upholds tradition and saves money so he can marry off his daughters well. Thus the cycle repeats and the fabric of life is woven.

Incredible India; it is vast, complex, a land of contrasts, with deserts, plains, snow-capped mountains, and the sea. It is traditional and modern, friendly and intrusive, secular and democratic, yet for the most part life is governed by religion and tribal law, where women are pampered or violated. It is the seat of the oldest continuous civilization, spiritual, the origin of four world religions, the center of ayurvedic healing and yoga, corrupt, rich in history and heritage sites, rich in potential, home to 1.2 billion people, and also home to the world's poorest of the poor. It is amazing, frustrating, numbing, confusing, overwhelming, satisfying, and inspirational. Incredible India.

"If you come to a fork in the road take it." – *Yogi Berra*

Hello, From Somewhere

CHAPTER 35: La Alberca

Day 1

Hola! I´m back in Spain after my Italian detour, and I finally was able to get into the Reina Sophia to view Picasso´s Guernica, which I missed the last two times I was in Madrid because the painting was on loan abroad. It is a complex work and Picasso had done numerous studies of the figures before assembling them, and it is a powerful image of the horror of war. I'm back to volunteer as an English speaker in the Pueblo Ingles immersion program for Spaniards. I met with my Anglo group at an introductory lunch, followed by Flamenco, before taking a four hour bus trip to Alberca. All of the people here are very interesting and very diverse; most of the Spaniards are young executives and managers in various industries, and there are several women.

Day 2

Now we're in the full schedule of the program, and it's no holiday. It is a stream of one-on-one sessions with just ten minute breaks in between, followed by group activities that are very structured to promote language use.

The resort villas are very nice, and we´re booked in private quarters with one Spaniard and one Anglo in each villa. I'm booked with a young woman who´s in sales and marketing. This evening I get to tell my jokes, but this is a pretty sedate and conservative lot so far. We're only just getting into the ice breakers, though, so we´ll see.

Day 3

The village is very charming indeed. We walked there during siesta, as that was the only part of the schedule where we had enough time to walk there and back. I got to tell my jokes, but only the clean ones, as this group so far appears to be a little uptight. My stand-up comic routine went over very well with the Anglos, but many of the Spaniards didn´t get the double meanings, so I discovered during later conversations at meal time. I found out the party animals at the bar in the evening, and we had a great time, dancing and shooting tequilas, so maybe things were going to be quite fun after all.

Day 4

We had an excursion to the village today. Alberca, formerly known as Valdelaguna, is located in the Southern part of the province of Salamanca. This village is 1,084 metres above sea level on the Northern slopes of 'la Sierra de Francia' (the French mountain range). Its unusual houses and streets have put it on the map for visitors to the province of Salamanca. This village was populated during the times of Alfonso VI by the French. In fact, some of its place names, like 'la Sierra de Francia' and 'el rio Frances,' reference these origins. Alberca's greatest asset is the diversity of the wonderful scenery that surrounds it. It is encircled by granite, slate and quartzite which support the varied wild vegetation and forests of oaks, chestnut trees, pine trees, walnut trees, apple trees and almond groves.

Like many other villages in Spain, Alberca's population is declining. Over half a century ago it had 1,700 inhabitants, but now this figure hardly reaches 1,000.The village is still well maintained, however, and despite harsh winters and very hot summers tourism plays an important part in its economy. Its narrow cobbled streets, small squares and curious houses make this a beautiful place to visit.

We finished our village tour in a bar and had drinking contest from a leather wine skin, the traditional bota, and cutting strips of the local delicacy, jamon iberico pata negra, from the bone, we filled our bota with more wine and sang and danced and promised to remember this happy time forever.

Day 5

I´m getting a lot from the jokes I can remember to tell correctly, and Ray just sent me a bar blonde joke which I certainly can find the right occasion to tell tonight. The one about the "bull winning too" has gotten many laughs here, and finally I got the right moment to tell the second opinion joke, about the surgeons wife, and some of Evelyn´s jokes.

Day 6

We´re winding down here, Friday we drive back to Madrid then I linger until the 28th and I should be seeing y'all in no time at all. I´m ready to go home. Tonight we´re rehearsing a comedy routine to present during pre-dinner entertainment. We´re drinking a lot of wine for lunch and dinner, I definitely will need to starve myself when I get home..

Rizal's Madrid

Dr. Jose Rizal, who lived from June 19, 1861 to December 30, 1896, was a Filipino polymath, nationalist and the most prominent advocate for reforms in the Philippines during the Spanish colonial era. He is considered the Philippines' national hero, and the anniversary of Rizal's death is commemorated as a Philippine holiday called Rizal Day. He was a student in Madrid as a member of the Ilustrados, the emerging Filipino educated class.

I got on the Line 2 metro and visited Rizal´s monument on La Avenida de las Filipinas. It was placed there during the Centennial of Philippine Independence in 1998, under Fidel Ramos' auspices. It´s on the corner of a new recreation park next to the Isabel II water reservoir, northeast of Madrid. It's a very nice park used by Madrilenos, just inaugurated last year, with a driving range and practice greens for golfers, soccer fields, fountains, resilient surfaced jogging paths, rose gardens, fountains, checker tables and chairs under trees. There's even a nice restaurant. I don´t know how many locals wonder who he is. They use the steps to stretch before running.

I checked out his addresses in Madrid on Barquillo Street and Cava San Miguel. There aren´t any plaque there about his stay. I had dinner in the San Miguel address No. 7, which is now a very funky bodega style restaurant. The whole street is very bohemian, and the restaurants there all have live music. It´s not too far from Puerta del Sol. I took the metro back as I´d wandered too far, and it was packed like sardines at 11:50 pm. Everybody in Madrid is just getting ready for the all night Saturday partying. I love Madrid.

I´m arriving in Atlanta at 2:30 PM tomorrow, see y'all soon!

CHAPTER 36 Australia

Hey mates!

My flight was smooth and arrived ten minutes early at 6:20 am, an amazing feat for DELTA. The sky was orange and red, and the view of Sydney on approach was spectacular. The whole world was arriving at the same time; they were unloading sixteen planes and customs and baggage queue was long but efficient. U.S. TSA inspected my checked suitcase and broke the latch even though I left it unlocked. I have to get a new suitcase, s---t. Xenia, my friend, was at the airport and promptly gave me a tour of the beaches. I'm staying in Coogee beach, and the famous Bondi is right next to it. The beaches are rapidly filled with bodies, as I've arrived on a Saturday. Like England, the driving here is on the left, and I'm nearly run over as I navigate the town. I'm waiting now to have dinner, and then watch "Cossi Fan Tutti" at the opera. I've already got plenty of recommendations on how I should see Australia.

Hi!

I have dedicated hosts who plan my Sydney experience scrupulously. We went to a car boot sale last Sunday, which is a community garage sale where you can sell all the goods that you can stuff in your car's trunk. I got real deals on a $2 sisal hat by Kangol, and a real Aussie hat for $20, plus my piece de resistance purchase, a sterling matchbox-size birthday book, with quotes from Shakespeare, Byron, etc. on each date page. I spent the afternoon at the beach then was invited to a barbecue at my friend's. Today my hotel host invited me to her nature walk group and we took a bus and the train to meet our walk party in the northern Sydney suburb, and hiked Primrose Park and the harbor coastline to view the expensive houses along it. There were swarms of wild cockatoos and parrots in the park. I can't get over how spectacular that was. In the afternoon, a friend I met on the walk took me on the ferry to Watson's Bay and to Gap Cliff for a magnificent view of Sydney harbor. We had lunch of fish and chips and Toohey beer. On our way back we got off the bus on Bondi beach and took the coastal walkway to Coogee. My hotel host will accompany me to Tasmania, a change of plans since they'd rather have me do that than schedule Adelaide.

Sydney is really the beaches. The city center is dark at night and nothing is going on there after dinner, but there's action on the beaches all night. The opera experience was fantastic. Tomorrow, my host will take me on a private tour of the city. I have great recommendations for the other places in my itinerary.
How was the Journey concert, did it get rained out?

Good day!

I'm not driving here because I could get killed; they drive like the English, on the wrong side. Even while jogging, you have to stay on the left. Runners have been giving me the arm signal to stay on my correct lane. The buses are efficient and take you directly to most places, so there's no need for taxis. I walked on the beach and stepped into the water but it was cold, so I just sunned and read.

The food is great here. I've had fish and chips for lunch three days in a row, and I've gotten to try their meat pies. They serve beetroot a lot, and the beetroot salad served by my friend is so delicious, roasted in olive oil and balsamic vinegar and whole garlic cloves. I'm going to copy it and serve on my next dinner party. I've had Thai for dinner (ethnic food is international) and a lunch of citrus-marinated sea trout with crab and caviar, and two dinners at friend's houses. It was barbecue at one, and at the other, soup of grilled salmon with udon noodles and bean sprouts and cilantro. My friend gave me a tour of the Sydney neighborhoods, the Rocks, which was the old settlement on the harbor. It is very charming, with restored colonial houses that have been turned into cafes and boutique shops. Town Hall, Darlinghurst and Paddington are all very chic and expensive, with row houses with wrought iron verandas like in New Orleans, King's Cross, and Oxford St., they're very bohemian, and look down on the circular quay with the iconic Sydney Opera, China town, and the QVB in the distance. The life style is laid back still, and people are very friendly. I'm open to meeting Crocodile Dundee when I get to the Outback. I'll be in Brisbane next.

Hi Mates!

After four days of marvelously perfect weather, we were struck by a thunderstorm last night, with hail in other parts of NSW.

All hell broke loose at 6 a.m. today after I arrived at the airport in Sydney. My early flight to Brisbane was cancelled and I'm rebooked four hours later, s__t! Mayhem, Armageddon! My rescheduled 11:05 a.m. flight was cancelled and I was rebooked to the 2:05 p.m. flight which was delayed and didn't leave until 6:05, so I didn't get to Brisbane until after 8 p.m. I heard something about a red dust storm, blowing from the Red Center in the Outback.

Hi Mates!

I'm in Brisbane finally but my luggage didn't arrive with me. With so many changes in flight schedule, this was bound to happen. My friend John was at the airport to pick me up, and the poor thing had to go back and forth because the airline won't give him confidential information. I arrived six hours after my original schedule. His wife, Jenny, had choir practice so he took me home first and fed me dinner and we picked her up after choir practice. I checked into my bed and breakfast, the Thornbury. It's a restored colonial cottage, a Queenslander, and it's very lovely. The dust storm weather preceded me in Brisbane, and I was worried we wouldn't be able to land. There's red dust covering everything, and even the natives haven't seen anything like this before. When I left Sydney, however, the sun was out and it looked like nothing was amiss, which was itself freaky. Tomorrow Jenny will take me around. I do not mind the delay at all. It was an adventure, and the Australians are a patient lot. They were all cheerful and good natured throughout the flight delays.

Got this email from Linda, "Armageddon hit Atlanta too. Guess you heard about our flooding. Spaghetti junction, downtown connector...glad I was in sunny Florida and missed it all! At least we had no red dust....just red clay that failed to absorb all the water."

G'day Y'all

I had Shabbat dinner last night with my Brisbane hosts, who are Jewish, and who are a very minor presence here. Brisbane is a nice, compact city with the river running through it, and is very pretty with lighted bridges and river promenades on both banks. They have a vibrant multi-use park on the south bank, a legacy of the 80's World Expo. Whereas Sydney has the beaches, Brisbane has the river. Its beaches are an hour away and very touristy with high rises and all, but they're long, uninterrupted, golden expanses of sand called the Gold Coast. But you have to be careful about jellyfish stings. I went to a Koala Sanctuary to see these fluffy critters up close and personal, but they're not so cuddly after all. And by the way, prostitution is legal here, and those who want to indulge will find ads of all types.

My suitcase arrived yesterday afternoon just in time for me to check out of Brisbane and take my flight to Darwin.

Ow ya mates!

Darwin, the top end as they call it here is hot and humid at 98F degrees today just like Hotlanta! I got reimbursed Au$60 for my luggage delay. Darwin is a small town, people just stay here to book trips to Kakadu and environs. Kakadu is a must but I'm also booking a tour of Tiwi Island, an aboriginal community. There are many tourists from other parts of Australia, but mostly from the UK.

The Northern territory is so close to Asia, the Asian cuisine here is fabulous. Indonesia is just above and the Philippine Seas not far. The Northern Territory gives acknowledgment to the aborigines as traditional owners of the land, but the White settlers are unhappy that they have entitlements from the government. I had somewhat of a jolt to see White folks doing the jobs we usually see done by Mexicans and Blacks in America, like construction, road work, housekeeping services in hotels, waiters , etc. Africans is a rarity, and aborigines are also a rarity in the cities. I'm beginning to stretch my a's,

G'day Mates!

The top end is heaven for the adventure traveler and backpacker, and one has to hike, climb, camp out, ply the waters, or go fishing, to appreciate the land. The Northern Territory is young and unsophisticated from the White settler perspective, but quite ancient and complex from the Aboriginal perspective, their rock paintings detailing their history is 40,000 years old. There are no slick hotels or resorts, or fine restaurants, but the ethnic cuisine is fabulous in variety and inexpensive. The city center is full of kids and backpackers, and I'm booked precisely there, well, I didn't do my research and accepted the recommendation of the, yes, the kid, at the tourist counter at the airport. I did ask for the center of action, so he did his job. There is a Crown Plaza in the business district but it's so quiet there after dark, and there are no accommodations on the water. I missed the best time to come, which would be just after the rains, when the wetlands is teeming with life, and water is gushing from the rivers and falls. Jim Jim falls is dry, but the river cruise still yielded many crocodile sightings and water birds.

Hi Mates!

I'm staying in this house of a friend of a friend of a friend in Port Douglas, one hour from Cairns, my room is a pavilion off to one end of a free flowing pool with cascading water into a moat at the base, it's on a hilltop surrounded by trees and three walls are all glass, the bathroom is all glass and overlooking a garden lush with tropical vegetation, you feel like you're taking a shower in the forest, and the view from the pool looks into the Coral Sea and the illusion of the pool connected to the sea is very dramatic. It's just the owner and I so we skinny dipped to complete the drama of being one with nature. I kept all the shades up in my room to bring in the great outdoors. Last night I had a gecko lining my toilet, and the noise of the forest kept me awake, various birds whistling or tweeting , cicadas, snorts and hisses, and the loud cackle and laughter of the kookaburra. I awoke to the sun rising on my right.

A full day of snorkeling the Great Barrier Reefs, went to three sites, incredible underwater display of brilliant fishes, convoluted coral forests in crayola, various creatures, and met Marvin a four-foot long gentle humphead Maori Wrasse, you can pat him on the head and swim with him, they are very territorial and Marvin had been guarding this particular location for a long time. Tomorrow I go to Daintree, the wet tropical rainforest, where I hope to sight a cassowary, the elusive, spectacular, ancient and endangered flightless bird.

Good day mates!

I am now in Alice Springs, gateway city to Australia's Red Center, where the outback legends still live and adventures abound. The red dust storm that paralyzed NSW and Queensland a few days ago that blanketed Canberra, Sydney, Brisbane, and Melbourne, making them look like Martian cities, and reduced temperatures and visibility and created havoc to air travel, and earned billing as Armageddon, started here, then blown all the way to New Zealand and dumped tons of dirt in Sydney Harbor. Slept under a shower of stars, and in the glow of campfire, listened to stories of cowboys, plucky pioneers, Afghan camel races, flying doctors, and gold diggers, and the laying of telegraph lines which opened the Red Center to the world. Our tour guide is a genuine cowboy who in his former life drove camels across the desert and knew personally wranglers, tricksters and all sorts of adventurers. Alas, he is no Crocodile Dundee. Saw wallabies and kangaroos in the wild. Sang Waltzing Matilda while we drove on Red Center Way, the road that cuts across the dramatic landscape of the desert outback. Impressed by the sight of Uluru, Ayers Rock, the red sandstone monolith rising from the desert. The sunset puts on a spectacular display of a changing kaleidoscope of colors and shadows on its surface. We accompanied the viewing with cocktails and wine. We hiked the Kings Canyon and Kata Tjuta. Returning to Alice Springs, I attended a didgeridoo concert, an aboriginal musical wind instrument, known in use for over 1500 years.

Hi Y'all

I'm staying in the condo of a friend of a friend, twenty minutes by train from the city center, and her neighborhood is gorgeous, has a little Main Street with shops and restaurants and services, very accessible. Melbourne is beautiful and well organized as a city with parks, compact city center and neighborhoods they call precincts. They have a large Greek community, second only to

Athens, and there's a Greek district in the city center, I had lamb dinner there tonight, and they also have a Chinatown and Little Italy, ethnic foods is a feast here, the shopping is diverse and avant garde, and the shopping districts are quite distinctive, especially the arcade shops and the markets. I got a fabulous silver cuff bracelet with a large Australian opal stone, and I can't help myself, bought another one from a local designer. The arts scene is very vibrant and there are many on-the-edge theater performances, too bad I don't have time to attend one. Tomorrow I take a trip down the Great Ocean Road, patterned after the California Pacific Coast Highway, and Friday I'm reserving to browse the huge and fabulous Victoria Market and to just get lost in all the nooks and crannies of the city. If I had the time, I'd play at the Rod Laver Tennis Center, which is open to the public. What's the scoop BTW with the Chris Evert and the Shark's split?

Last night my host had dinner guests and we had great conversation about being Australian, and considered the world's problems and their solution over bottles of great wines from the great Australian vineyards. It is exciting to be Australian these days, I can feel it from everyone's attitude, they are optimistic, forward looking and very proud of how far they've come. Did you know that their national coat of arms is a shield and two animals, the kangaroo and the emu, why these two? because these animals are incapable of taking steps backwards, they can only go forward, and that's how Australians believe they do.

Ow ya goin'

I didn't get any sighting of a Tasmanian devil, I learned they are in danger of extinction in the wild due to a virus infecting their mouths, but I got educated about Tassie's ignoble convict past at Port Arthur. Tasmania is picture card perfect with snow capped mountains and green hills with Victorian cottages with English gardens spilling into the harbor filled with sailboats, fishermen hauling in catch at the pier, farms heavy with produce, eggs so tasty with more colorful yolks, vineyards putting out the most delicate pinot noirs, and great beers made with clear waters from Mt. Wellington. We got in on a Saturday and the Salamanca market was very colorful. My new friend from Sydney joined me, and we stayed in this turn of the century B&B in a suite that's decorated with the exact fixtures and furnishings of a cabin in the Titanic, filled with Titanic memorabilia, quite fun, this is at Battery point, with a view of the harbor and just a block from their main activity center, Salamanca place. Not much going on at night though unless you're a backpacker and hanging out at the pubs, so we went to see Elvis Costelo, never heard his music before.

Before I left Melbourne, Harry Connick was a guest at this reunion broadcast of a popular variety show twenty years ago and they had a blackface number which Harry commented on as not politically correct, and it was in the news for several days with panels and comments from all sides. They have racial issues here which they are still in denial of. It's not all roses in paradise.

Well I'm back in Sydney now, and will be home soon.

CHAPTER 37: Israel, Egypt, Jordan

Nile

On the shore of Lake Victoria, in Tanzania four years ago, I was overcome with an expansive feeling while contemplating that here I am at the headwaters of the Nile, the longest river in the world, the source of life that gave birth to the glorious civilization of ancient Egypt. Someday I will visit and see for myself what this life source had created.

We boarded our Nile cruiser, the Medea in Aswan after taking the overnight sleeper train from Cairo. The train ride offered a glimpse of how crowded Cairo is. The hoi polloi massed to overflowing in the coach section, while thankfully we had our private cabins.

It was suddenly very hot when we arrived in Aswan. Cruising the Nile offers a vast landscape of golden wheat fields and goats grazing and graceful date palms, mud houses and children playing, a narrow swath of green, then the arid desert beyond. Along its shore also lie the tombs of kings and temples to gods that survived for over thousands of years, monuments that give awe and inspiration, that man through all times is capable of brilliant invention and creativity. The creations also testify to man's folly and cruelty, and to his need for immortality and salvation.

Of Gods and Men

Egyptian archaeological treasure is immense. The Cairo Egyptian Museum, opened in 1909, houses thousands of artifacts in an aging building that's dusty and not air-conditioned. Its wood and glass exhibit cases, with notes typewritten in an old Corona typewriter, are relics themselves. The Tutankhamun treasures alone occupy one large wing, and only a small sample is exhibited at a time. King Tut's gleaming golden mummy mask is jaw-droppingly awesome, and that's just the beginning. Giza, with the Sphinx and the Pyramids, is on the outskirts of Cairo. You can see it from the city, and the juxtaposition of images is poetry. Four-thousand years ago, before soot and smog blemished the polished white limestone surface of the pyramids, it rose from the desert landscape as an iridescent apparition visible from miles away. And the Valley of the Kings is so immense; over sixty tombs have been identified. It's impossible to imagine what it was like in its own time. The pharaohs had the vision, but the peasants and slaves produced the artistry and know-how that erected these everlasting monuments that have lasted over 5000 years.

Cairo

My flight to Egypt from Israel arrived around 2:30 am, and getting a taxi from the airport was a hassle because there is no ground transportation counter and rates are not posted. You have to rely on your instincts to avoid being fleeced. I shared a taxi with a young couple winging it on their own, and found out later we made a good bargain. There were only twenty passengers from Israel, but when we deplaned in Cairo there was a multitude emptying from another flight. They were in galabiyyas and veils and turbans and were reeking of body odor, jostling their way into the exit after passport control without order, first-come, first-served. What a contrast from the disciplined order at Ben Gurion airport. I didn't know where the people came from, but they were pushing loads of cargo bursting with thick comforters, big plastic bags of clothes pulled together with ropes, and heaps of luggage. It seemed there was no baggage limit on whatever plane they were on. It certainly beats the balikbayans and their boxes at Nionoy Aquino airport.

I checked into Marriott Omar Khayyam, fabulous, a former palace, all gilt and lavish carvings and appointments, there's a small casino too, but it's obviously for the tourists, as Muslims prohibit gambling.

The Cairenes are very friendly but pretty soon I realize it is for the tourist dollars, so I don't know how friendly they really are. The modus operandi is; they ask where you're from, then say they know somebody from where you're from, then pretty soon if you give them time they tell you their sad stories and expect a hefty tip afterwards. Well, the economy is bad, and with a city of twenty million people they have to survive in whatever way they can. But the offers of help or whatever else are so insistent and in your face that they lose their playfulness very quickly. Cairo is covered in soot and dust and the buildings are decaying. The Egyptians also have a peculiar custom of leaving the top floor of their houses unfinished with the steel rods exposed, for future finishing when the sons get married. It doesn't hurt that they don't have to pay taxes until the building is completed, so the mass housing all around the city looks unfinished or ruined.

The Cairo cemetery is old and huge, and there are people living among the graves, a city among the dead. Aside from the government buildings and old palaces and high end hotels along the Nile, Cairo is a city of rubble and mass housing in perpetual construction.

However, seeing Cairo again after being away for a few days and looking at the city from the air, where I cannot see the soot and rubble of the slums, and without the press of the hoi polloi, and the smell of the body odor and the fumes, I can see that the city was once beautiful, with the Nile cutting a shimmering swatch in the middle, and banked by palaces and magnificent mosques and gardens. It almost looks like Paris. In colonial times the Brits must have lived a grand life indeed, with the Egyptians serving tea and moving the breeze with hand held fans.

Egyptians like to think of themselves as a distinct people and not lumped with the Arabs. Many Muslims are Arabs, but not all Muslims are Arabs. Israelites are also a diverse group. They are mostly Jews, but there are Arabs, the Bedouins, and Druze who were grandfathered as Israelites when Israel became a nation. Among Jews, there are the Hasidic, Ashkenasians, and Sephardic. Then there are the tourists.

The food here is healthy and essentially Mediterranean cuisine, with lots of grilled lamb, chicken or fish, and grilled vegetables marinated in olive oil and vinegar. Eggplants are my favorites in particular. A grilled eggplant and tomato salad with garlic, olive oil and vinegar is reminiscent of a Filipino dish that I love.. There are smoked or pickled fish and cabbage in many variations. Meze, among the Arabs, covers an infinite variety of appetizers, very much like tapas. Of course, there's kebab, shawarma (gyro), tahini, falafel, pita, and black coffee with cardamom. There's baklava, matzo, gefilte fish, lots of and plenty of dates and nuts. There's no pork or shellfish, as they're prohibited under Jewish and Muslim dietary laws, and while Israel has some very good wines, the Muslims don't drink. The cheese selection here is also limited.

I had dinner of grilled pigeon, a delicacy. The domestic birds are kept in backyard pigeon houses for grilling or stuffing with spicy rice. It was delicious, but it was hard work to eat because there's barely any meat attached to the bones. Meanwhile, I stared at a burqa-clad woman as she slipped her food under the veil. I'd go hungrier eating this way.

Jordan, Amman

Jordan is a country about to join the tourist trade. There is construction aimed at tourists all over. The pink city of Petra and Moses' mountain and the baptism site of Jesus, are some of antiquities here. The bulk of Amman, however, is a new city with many shopping malls and a residential district for the rich and powerful and their million-dollar houses. There is a huge development in the middle of the city between the old district and the new which, like Atlantic Station, is a city in itself. The Middle East is not merely building skyscrapers, it is building cities with projected populations of up to 2 million. The UAE, Abu Dhabi, Dubai, Saudi Arabia and even Qatar are all building mega cities from the ground up.

The wage here averages 300 Jordanian dinar ($1.30 to JD1) per month, so life here is tough for the middle class. Cars are expensive, and the affordable car for the populace is made in Korea. There are Palestinian settlements in the old city and it creates friction, but 42% of Jordanians are from Palestine and many are related. Individuals weigh in on the Palestine/Israel conflict based on their personal relations. The newspapers have news about a journalist arrested for criticizing the parliament. Filipino female domestic workers are blacklisted here because some entrepreneur brought them in and had them work as prostitutes. Why they did not arrest the entrepreneur is another story.

CHAPTER 38: Ireland

Sept 17-October 10, 2011

We've been here in Meath for just forty-eight hours but it feels like we've done a lot already. We arrived in time to witness Dublin win the all-Ireland football championship against Kerry, something that has eluded them for sixteen years, so the city was wild with celebration. We were warned not to make the forty minute trip to Dublin from our hotel in Meath because the city would be crazy. Well, we wanted crazy, so we went and had a grand time celebrating with the locals. We did the pub crawl and the Guinness was flowing. I had to hold on to my red Kangol beret as it was snatched from my head a few times, I don't know why since the winning color was Dublin blue.

Yesterday we were in Drogheda and entered Ollie's Pub around 3 p.m. to fortify ourselves for the 56-step climb to the Millmount Tower. There were only men inside and all eyes were upon us. As we took our seats a guy approached us all friendly and puppy-like. He introduced himself and then boasted that talking with us made him the bravest man in the room. Well, we were the toast of the pub for the time it took to finish a pint of Guinness.

The Irish are story tellers, as everyone knows, and we were held captive by Owens, the guy at the Tourist Bureau who had us enthralled with trivia and tales about the place. He gave us good recommendations for restaurants, and being a golfer he told us to introduce ourselves to Bobby Brown, the pro, and Richard, the bartender at Bettystown Golf Club where we would be golfing the next day. We casually invited him to join us for lunch, and he indeed stopped by while we were at Stockwell Artisan Foods. Did he surprise us, though, when he left his lunch bill for us to pay.

Oh well, he was charming and all of his recommendations were excellent, so we considered it his tip.

Marci and I enjoyed golf at Laytown and Bettystown Club. It was 56 degrees F, sunny for four holes, drizzling for the next three holes, then suddenly sunny again for a couple of holes and cloudy the rest of the way. The course featured dunes and tight fairways, wind and the Irish sea. We got lost finding the next holes, since they were sparsely marked, and had to ask for directions from the other golfers, who were all very obliging and charming. Kathy went on the Tara hop-on, hop-off shopping tour. We have the Solheim Cup scheduled for Friday.

September 23, 2011

It is said that the people of Ireland are genuinely friendly, and I don't doubt it. "Much obliged," and "no problem at all," are the common responses to any request, and even if I am referred to as "luv", it does not seem sexist at all. Children here can still venture out of their yard to play, and people chat easily that I feel like we're best friends after our conversation. Life in these villages hark back to a time that had become relegated to nostalgia.

It is unbelievable that we're coming to the end of our week here. We saw the USA team lose to Europe today on the first day of the Solheim Cup competition. Tomorrow, Kathy will join her family arriving in Dublin for a wedding and I will hitch a ride with Paddy, a genuinely friendly Irish who will take me along to Belfast since he was going there for a christening anyway, no problem at all. I will rendezvous with my Ireland in Depth Tour and Marci has a flight back to Atlanta on Sunday.

September 25, 2011- Belfast

It is amazing that Belfast can go on like a normal city, considering that the Good Friday Agreement for cease fire from sectarian violence, commonly referred to as "The Troubles", was only passed in 1998. From the late 1960's to as recently as 2001, bombings, kidnappings, and terrorism have been facts of daily life .But from the rubble and ashes, it has emerged like the phoenix, and life in the city center pulsates with energy. The wound still smarts, the population is still divided, and walls still exist to maintain the peace, but it is transforming its tragedy into opportunity. These walls are tourist attractions now, and from the remains of its linen factories and shipbuilding graveyard, it is completing a harbor-side tourism center with the Titanic Museum as its centerpiece. There you go; economics is the certain agent for peace. And the ultimate irony is that these days, Belfast is designated as the second safest city in the world for tourism after Tokyo.

Derry

We drove on the scenic Causeway Coastal Route from Belfast to Londonderry/Derry, the UK City of Culture 2013. The double name of this gateway city to Ireland's northwest reflects the sectarian division that continues to be a fact of life for residents of this historic 17th century walled city. Like Belfast, this city is still reconciling with the infamy of the Troubles. It continues to stir passionate partisan affiliations, and how you name this city identifies who you sleep with. The Nationalists call it Derry, and the Unionists, Londonderry. Our tour guide who is Irish is clearly on the side of the Nationalists and as it is presidential election year, the news is inundated with candidates' propaganda, representing divergent positions in relation with the UK, that was too complicated for me. But I got acquainted with Michael Collins, the father of Irish Independence, a swashbuckling figure.

CHAPTER 39: Peru

February 4-28, 2011

Hola!

I've just landed in Lima. Customs was a breeze, with very pleasant clerks and lots of counters. My luggage came with me, thank goodness. The last time I was in this part of the hemisphere, in Ecuador, my luggage went to Bogota and never got to me until I returned to Atlanta, minus my new leather backpack. It's summer here, and I peel off my sweatshirt. I have to recheck my luggage to Cuzco, and the first flight out is at 5:45 this morning. I got here at 12:20 a.m., so I'm hanging out here at Starbucks. There's no time difference, direct flight is under 7 hours, and Cuzco is in the highlands, so it should be cooler there.

Bienvenudos!

It hardly snows in Cuzco, but the altitude makes me feel like I'm on the ski slopes. I have a slight headache, but acclimatizing shouldn't be a problem. My host steeps coca leaves into a drink to make me forget any discomfort, and with so many uses, I could easily become addicted. My host family is great, They don't speak any English, and for the past twenty-four hours I've been having conversations only in Spanish, and through broken grammar we've gotten acquainted and I'm sure I'll get better speaking it every day. That's my reason for volunteering in this Spanish immersion program. Did you think I'd gone soft and gone into charitable goody-goody work? I have to pay to volunteer in this program. It has many offices all over the world and many in Latin America, so I figured that if I liked it I could continue my Spanish language program with them.

From the airport Cuzco looks derelict, with rubble and trash on the streets and abandoned construction projects, but the historical city center, the hub of tourism, is quite charming, with hilly narrow cobblestone alleys, Spanish tile rooftops, and antique churches framed by the sky and the mountains. The Indians come to the city from the highlands in their colorful costumes to make money off the tourists by selling woven items, paintings, leather, etc. Llamas are strolling through the car and bus traffic. I took a photo of this kid with his burro, after which he extended his hand for a propina. Oh well, the tourists have educated him already. Plaza de Armas is full of tourists. It was drizzling this afternoon, but as soon as the showers stopped, people streamed into the plaza and filled the benches. There are wonderful restaurants that I need to try very soon, for lomo saltado and grilled guinea pig, llama, alpaca, goat, etc. The boutiques lining the plaza are stocked with beautifully designed silver and stone jewelry, alpaca apparel, leather goods that are to die for. These designer items are very expensive, in the same price range as those of NYC high-fashion houses, so I opted to stay alive. I did buy an alpaca sweater from the Indians for 40 Nuevo Sol, about $15.

Buen dia!

Rik, the Peru country coordinator who is from Holland, took me out to dinner for orientation at Marcelo Batabata restaurant where I had grilled alpaca with Peruvian chili sauce. Alpaca meat is touted to have many health benefits, being very lean with healthy fats and antioxidants. Where it was the staple for the highland Indians, it has now become beyond the reach of ordinary folks, and only the tourists can afford to eat it. It is very lean, and I ordered it medium. It has a bland taste, not gamey at all, but was ultimately forgettable. I've had lomo saltado, and the dish takes me back home, it is exactly as I remember, with strips of beef sauteed in onions, julienne carrots and potatoes and peas. I am awaiting recommendations for the best place to go for cuy, guinea pig. The young Dutch women with me in the same home-stay, they are the adventurous sort, dreamy and blonde, have already tried it. They did not rave about it.

I am in a one-on-one intensive Spanish course for two hours a day. My opening session with Jose Renzo, my instructor, gave me a headache. We had non-stop conversation on a wide array of topics ranging from food to politics. He corrected me as we went along, and paused to expand on some grammatical points, and that was my class. I like the method, and I'm looking forward to my next session.

The Meeting Place, a cafe which is run as a non-profit to support some children's and women's shelter is a gathering place for the international youth volunteers. One of the blondes will be volunteering in a program in Iquitos, in the Amazon, to work with children to encourage them to attend schools. It is run by two women from Holland. The San Blas School, where I'm taking my language class, is co-owned by a Dutch who married a local woman, the daughter of my hosts. There are also a lot of German youth in the volunteer corp. In the café all I overhear are conversations about program funding and charitable works being launched by individuals. What is going on here with all these charity good deeds by the Europeans?.

Cuzco, outside of the historic center, is poor, and the majority population is indigenous. My host family is considered wealthy by local standards, but there's no running hot water except the shower, which can turn cold in the middle of sudsing. They hardly eat out and the premises are very basically furnished. They don't go to theaters or have drinks at a bar. The children have some college, but they're not in a profession. Tourism is a major industry here, and my host's children are working in it. I have ambivalent feelings about all the good people from foreign countries doing non-sectarian charity works here. Not to exclude those who are here to proselytize religion. They are all the same to me. It makes me think of colonial Philippines, christianized under 300 years of Spanish rule, and Americanized under fifty years of US imperialism. Spain killed the Filipino soul, America exhumed it in Hollywood.

By the way, one has to be sensitive here about how you use the word "America." If asked where you're from, it's offensive to say "I'm American," because that's co-opting all the Americas, North and South and Center. If asked I should answer, "Soy de estados unidos." However, people actually are asking about my ethnicity, and not my citizenship or residence, so I say, "Soy de filipinas."

Abrazos y Besos!

I had a most amazing day! Without language proficiency, I am useless in the clinic I'm supposed to work in and the sisters don't know what to do with me. I got the feeling I'm just a nuisance. There are dozens of patients in the downstairs waiting hall, and Sister Paulina's computer is acting up and she has an IT person there trouble shooting it. She has no time to orient me and to find a department for me to work in where my language limitation will not be a factor. She asked me if I wanted to accompany her to visit a clinic in the mountain. She has some parochial business to attend to in Zurite, with Sister Matilde and Father Nicanor. It is over an hour's drive from Cuzco. Before driving out of the city we stopped for a bag of coca leaves. I'm apprised that chewing them will help us adjust to the altitude. The indigenous people rely on it to give them energy while working the fields all day, and it also helps to curb hunger.

When we arrived in Zurite, we queued behind one of the service windows in the municipal building. I found out they wanted to meet with the mayor, but he wasn't in. They showed up without giving advance notice, not minding whether or not the person is in. Sounds familiar? It's very much like the Philippines here. People take their time for appointments, getting there when they get there. The mayor will be back in the afternoon, and in the meantime we went to see another person. We drove through very narrow dirt roads bordered by low shacks constructed of bricked straw and clay with Spanish tile roofs. Then we came to a better constructed house and knocked for a long time, without success. We went back to the municipal building and stood in line again, but this time only briefly, for the alcalde, Alberto Tuco, came out and received us.

My hosts were paying their respects to the new mayor, because they have a school there. They also run free medical clinics twice a month, the only medical care available in these mountain villages. By this time it was 2 pm and I had already missed my lunch with the girls, my Spanish class, and by how it was going I would also miss my appointment with the tour operator who was preparing my travel itinerary after I complete my volunteer work. I was also wondering if we'd ever have lunch. The coca leaves sure were working for them, but not for me. Along the way, we took a detour for my benefit. They wanted to show me a seldom-visited site of impressive Inca ruins, the Tarawasi piedras. Then finally we stopped for lunch in this tiny roadside restaurant. There was only one dish on the menu, whatever fixings were available from the farm that day. The meal was typical but surprisingly very sophisticated. There's always a primera and a segunda. The first was a corn soup thickened with potato and filled with Lima beans and carrots, the broth very nuanced in flavor. The second was braised beef shank with peas, potatoes, carrots and rice. I'm told there are 1,300 plus varieties of potatoes in Peru, so it figures in every meal. A condiment accompanying every meal is the Peruvian chili sauce, Aji. It wakes up all the flavors. I offered to pay for lunch, and I couldn't believe it. The whole thing, four lunches with chamomile tea with anise for beverage, costs 16 soles, or $6.

But the surprise didn't end there. We took another detour and drove up a steep hill on narrow dirt and washed out road. The vehicle was groaning, and I was wondering how we were going to turn around to go back. They took me to an Inca site not yet opened to tourists. It is the Killia Raymi, an amazing half-moon carved into thick stone. It is aligned with some point in the heavens and had something to do with lunar rituals. I didn't get back to Cuzco until dark, and had to make apologies for my absence. On second thought, I didn't miss my Spanish class. I had seven hours of Spanish conversation today.

Hola!

The poor are the same all over the world, and the rich too. The big difference is between the rich and the poor. Charity, volunteer and missionary work is an industry here. I suppose it's a win-win situation, the haves get their gratification of whatever motives they have in working with the poor and the poor get bread, shelter, shoes, and indebtedness. For an exceptional few, they get opportunity for a different life. Whether they're better off or not is the question for Solomon.

Anyway, there's nothing useful for me to do in the clinic. I missed my Spanish classes while taking these all-day trips to the mountains so I renegotiated my assignment. Donating money rather than my time would help the clinic more, which is in dire need of basic medical supplies. All agreed that I would conclude my clinic assignment after one week so I could make up my missed Spanish classes in the second week. In exchange for my volunteer work, I gave a donation of supplies to the clinic.

In the meantime Sister Matilde, who practices alternative medicine and who compounds the clinic's repertoire of herbal treatments, gave me a primer on native medicinal plants and how they are used to treat a myriad of ailments. It was most fascinating and priceless. She lets me help in her laboratory, mixing dried herbs, bagging them and labeling and shelving them. Patients come in for consultation and she dispenses the treatment. She also fills prescription for outside doctors. I will do bagging for one more day, then I'm done with volunteering. We've become friends, however, and I have an open invitation to lodge in their community house should I return to Cuzco. She offered to arrange a stay with her family in Ariquipa since I'm visiting there. We are also going to the theater tonight to see a performance of Peruvian folk dances. Sister Paulina, who is the director of the clinic, invited me to their staff lunch tomorrow. I'm happy, they're happy.

Queridas,

It was raining in Cusco at midnight when I got back from Machu Picchu, and the taxi driver charged me double to get home from the bus stop, mierda!

Hola!

I've been cut off from the rest of the world without cellular reception and WiFi in the Amazon rainforest and in Lake Titicaca. While the Arab world is in the throes of cataclysmic change, in these two places life goes on pretty much the same every day, only concerned with the basics of living. In Lake Titicaca, the pre-Incan indigenous tribes in the three Islands we visited still keep their centuries old traditions in spite of 300 years of Spanish colonial rule. Lake Titicaca, the highest navigable lake in the world, sits on Puno with an elevation of 12,421 feet compared to Aspen's 7,950 feet. I've been extremely short of breath trekking in these mountains and climbing hills, and my lingering cough does not help. In Amantani, where we had an overnight home stay, we dressed in traditional costumes, which the natives wear every day and attended their community dance.

The Amazon jungle is immense and teeming with life, but unlike my African safari, the animals are not visible. We woke up at 4 am just to catch a glimpse of them.

We were lucky to spot two species of monkeys, a family of otters, a few birds of prey, and a spectacular clay lick of macaws, parakeets, tucans, and parrots. We cast a line for piranhas, and they were biting, but I didn't catch any. It rained every day, a light drizzle for the most part with occasional brief downpours, but it was warm so we just ignored the rain and didn't interrupt our program. The Amazon lodge is open to the jungle, and there was a red howler monkey outside my room. There are strict ecotourism policies in the Amazon, and we're not allowed to feed or disturb the animals, lest they start bothering people. The visit to a local shaman was interesting. Naturally, I was the first to try para-para, an aphrodisiac, but it had no effect.

CHAPTER 40: Indochina Holiday

Hello!

Left Atlanta on February 29 for a fourteen-hour flight to Narita, then to Bangkok arriving on March 2 at 5:20 am at Suvarnabhumi International Airport. I watched six movies on board, "Ides of March", "My Week with Marilyn", "Bridesmaids", "The Descendants". I watched "Hangover 2" just to feast on Bradley Cooper and see the locations filmed in Thailand. The rest of the movie you can skip. I also saw "Anonymous" which is about Shakespeare not being the author of all those plays. The moon was over our wing, and the city below was shimmering in gold and white lights as we landed. The airport was mobbed with planes unloading simultaneously. Susan and Niti were waiting for a long time because immigration control took more than an hour, even if I didn't queue in the visa line, as US nationals are exempt from visa requirements.

So we slept until noon until it was time for our massage appointment, which I needed after that twenty-hour flight. Massages and spas shouldn't be missed while visiting here. The Health Center is a huge facility with eight branches in Bangkok and offers body wraps, aromatherapy, facials, reflexology and massages. For a complete body makeover I think the ultimate is Thai massage. We had a two-hour session and nothing was left tight in my body at the end. OK, even my you-know-what was relaxed.

I only wanted to do the things Niti and Susan do on ordinary days, saving the temples and palaces and sights for my tour guide. So we spent the rest of the day at Siam Paragon, the Pride of Bangkok, a mega mall that surpasses all of the mall experiences I've had so far, including the Mall of America and Mega Mall of Manila, (Dubai Mall excluded).

It is a high end mall like Phipps Plaza and more, with all the mega designers: Balenciaga, Dior, Chloe, Hermes, Prada, Versace, you name it. Their stores and displays are huge, and the merchandise selection is more varied.

There are international jewelers, with Cartier, van Cleef & Arpels, etc. There are, sections for local designers with great styles, furniture, books, and art galleries. You can even buy a Ferrari and a custom car for $800,000. There is a fast food mega-section where you can feast on fresh food to order with mind-boggling variety at stupendous bargain prices of a mere 50-90 Baht, about $2-4. There's a sweets alley with offerings to die for, and French macarons are all over. There is even a supermarket.

On the top floor, there's a bowling alley and lounge surrounded by intimate karaoke rooms and a cinema showing mostly American movies. In the basement there's Siam Ocean World, a huge underground aquarium with 30,000 creatures swimming. It hosts exhibits, activities like diving and swimming with the sharks, IMAX, etc. And the complex is rimmed by a promenade surrounded by water. There are fountains and reflecting pools within, and the whole place is gleaming in steel, marble and glass. In the evening, as this opulent show for Bangkok's 1% closes its doors, the streets become alive in the night market, where the 99% of Bangkok's population shops and eats.

Buddhas, Street Dining, Canals

It was so hot today, and the protocol of viewing temples required covering skin, so naturally I was soaked in sweat. I heard about the tornadoes sweeping through the US and Georgia. I hope everyone is okay. There was flooding in Bangkok just before I arrived, and though it was far from the city center, it did not spare the houses lining the banks of the Chao Phraya River and its canals. The brief river cruise offered some cooling respite. From there we scanned Chinatown, Indiatown, and many wholesale markets, which are all teeming with people. The markets are all very crowded, always open. When brick and mortar shops close, the street markets and the night markets take over. Nothing compares to oriental markets in the bustle and variety and in the capacity to surprise.

CHAPTER 41:It's More Fun in the Philippines

Hi Y'all!

I can't believe I have another dental emergency on the road. I broke a tooth at breakfast and thank goodness I found a nice young dentist, Dr. Oliver L. Seno, who fixed it in no time at all. I just had a tooth pulled in Las Vegas on New Year's eve and wrangling that service was a networking feat. I am now in Cebu and scheduled to take a ferry to Bohol to meet Delia. Tooth repaired, I still had some free time for a quick tour of the city. All's well that ends well, and the Force is with me.

There's a planeful of South Koreans on my flight. Cebu is inundated with them, as students enrolled in proliferating English language schools and as tourists. I remember seeing them all over Boracay and at my golf trip too. In fact, locals soliciting massages or hair braiding on the beaches ask you in Korean now. The Saudi *balikbayans* have been dethroned. It used to be that if you were in Divisoria, they ask if you're visiting from Saudi. The *balikbayans* from the USA have been third rate tourists at least since the past decade, and their dollar is not as green anymore. It's a fact that overseas workers remittance accounts for 10.4% of the Philippines GDP.

I've been reading the paper and the presidential candidates either have criminal or ethical charges. A senator fled the country to avoid murder charges. Though election is not until May and campaigning is not official until this month, Villar is closing the gap fast with Noynoy and would you believe that Erap is pulling 13% in the polls? Only in the Philippines can a convicted felon and raider of the national treasury run for President again. He was pardoned by his successor and deemed squeaky clean again. The masses continue to idolize him , seeing him as the hero of his past macho movies, and ignore the reality of his character. A *calesa* driver I asked said he'll vote for Erap, and I asked why, he simply said that when Erap was president, he could feed his family better. The hoi polloi does not care who is governing, he only wants to have a good job and opportunity. And Erap's campaign pitch understands that too well, "rice in every pot".

Karaoke bars have stopped playing Sinatra's "My Way" because the song apparently had accounted for assaults and six killings so far. I'm getting weary of the diffident and subservient manner of the service personnel who deals with the tourist directly, the bellhops, drivers, waiters, reception staff, and the vague and indirect ways people communicate. I am also disappointed with the way history is presented to the tourist. Cebu and Bohol, where the Spaniards first landed, are rich with historical landmarks of the colonization, but the guides only address the arrival of the Spaniards. I wish this were an opportunity to educate about our rich pre-Hispanic heritage, and I wish travel agencies would emphasize the indigenous culture. Advertising is so over the top, with typical Filipino bombast and exaggeration, and you arrive and become disenchanted because the reality does not match the promise. I'd rather be surprised in the other direction. I think tourism here needs regulations about truth in advertising. Anyway, I'm a hard critic because I want tourism to be a seamless and really a fantastic experience here without apologies.

The country, however, is beautiful, the beaches and sea breeze are relaxing, the food is fantastic, and shopping is peerless.

I'm staying at the new Parklane Hotel here, near the new Ayala Mall. Cebu is constructing skyscrapers everywhere.

Barangay Adecor

I was battling some intestinal virus after leaving Bohol, and it made me really cranky (and crappy), but now my bowels are back under control. Was it my change in attitude? I went into Zen mode and swayed wherever the breeze blew, like the palm trees dancing on the pearly shores of Pearl Farm.

I wanted to leave the resort and walk to the nearby barangay, and they sent a security guard to escort me. I was joined by a Pearl Farm employee getting off from her work in the kitchen who lived in the barangay. They are very friendly and simple people, grateful that they are working at the resort. There was a town hall meeting in the basketball plaza, when we arrived. They were planning the upcoming fiesta of their patron saint, St Vincent. They have a little chapel, and there's a priest who comes to say mass every other Sunday. He makes the rounds of all the *barangays in* the remote islands. Karaoke singing was blaring in one section of the *barangay* and there were men drinking San Miguel and having a ball. They obviously were not attending the town hall meeting. On the beach, six men were singing a capella while fashioning the skeleton of a boat.

Locally made from indigenous materials and fitted with outboard motors, boats like these can be made very cheaply and yet remain very sea worthy. Butuan in Cotabato is where they found the remains of pre-Hispanic boats that sailed around the Southeast and reached as far as Madagascar. This seafaring culture of pre-HIspanic Philippines is being celebrated by the Balangay voyage project, spearheaded by those dreamers who scaled Mt Everest four years ago. I was so enamored by this venture that I continue to follow the voyage and sent monetary support. Google Balangay voyage further, it is so inspiring. Anyway, this small *barangay* here continues the tradition of hand-crafted boats.

Abject poverty is found in the urban areas. Here in the province, food is plentiful, people plant vegetables and flowers, they build boats cooperatively, *bayanihan* style, they weave fish nets, they tend fish corrals, and everyone has shelter fashioned from *nipa* and coconut fronds. In those little *nipa* huts I can see the flicker of TV screens, and they plan weekend events like disco at the plaza and basketball and karaoke-fests. Then there's the annual fiesta of course, not to mention religious holidays celebrated throughout. Children look healthy and happily chase dogs and each other. They look at you shyly, but two pretty little girls allowed me to take a photo of them hugging each other, best friends forever. This one lady has lived here over twenty years, and she knows the history of the place. The *barangay* name Adecor is from the Aguinaldo company that operated a real pearl farm here years ago. When the pearl business closed shop the people elected to stay, and then the place was transformed into the current resort, which is the main employer of the area.

There are 1800 registered voters in the *barangay*. I wonder how many will be counted in the election. There is so much concern expressed about the communications being jammed to prevent electronic transmission of votes for counting, this being the first instance of electronic voting here. There are also many worries about whether or not the masses can operate the machines correctly, having no experience with computers, and GMA is threatening to extend her reign if the elections cannot be declared properly counted, etc. She is running for councilor in her district, says there's nothing barring her in the constitution, and of course she'll win. She has showered the district with pork barrel projects and her picture is attached to all of these. In fact, her picture is attached to all that's happening all over the Philippines in the remote barrios. Her picture is the only politician's billboard, identifying the project as a project of GMA for the benefit of the people, from roads, new airports, ports, scholarships, agriculture, everything that a government should be doing is identified with her alone, oh well.

Paddling the Puerto Princesa Subterrenean River

It's already an adventure to get to the mouth of the cave where the underground river comes out to empty into the sea, and where tourists board paddle *bancas* to take them into the belly of Hades. I asked the cave guide if we can turn off the spotlight so I can see how dark it is (oxymoron?). Nope, can't do it, but if I close my eyes, he advised, that would answer my question, *tusong* Pinoy! The chambers are huge, the limestone formations eerie, and the river water is emerald green. In one chamber, named the Cathedral, the ceiling was very high and bats hung on jutting formations, in slumber. Cave swallows twittered as they flew to find their way by reflected sound, water dripped from the ceiling, and pitter-pattered on the flowing river and sent keplock echoes in the chamber, and then suddenly a spotlight disturbing the ambience, caused by a pack of returning tourists. The guide posed a question, what name do you call the bat youngling? *Bata*, heh heh.

The cave is stunning.

It took two hours by bus to get to the other side of Palawan, as Puerto Princesa is on the Sulu Sea side in the east and the river empties into the South China Sea in the west. Then in Sabang, it took a twenty-minute motorboat ride in the open sea to reach the entrance to the cave. Along the way we saw the lush Palawan countryside, farms and farmers, rain forests, limestone cliffs, mahogany and cashew trees. We made a pit stop for the toilets in a viewing area which also sold coffee and pearls. Fresh water pearls are practically being given away here, and the real McCoy South Sea Pearl costs a pittance. Then after we got out of the cave we had lunch in Sabang, where the beach is golden and the water hangs at 30 degrees celsius. We swam until it was time to return. Our guide was having a *Tamilok* ceviche, the mangrove worm, but I dare not try it. My good defense is I'm still recovering from intestinal virus.

Island Hopping on Honda Bay

There are more than a dozen islets and sandbars that are scattered in Honda Bay, but most tour operators take you to three islands for beaching and snorkeling, or diving. There's Starfish Island, Bat Island, Cowrie Island, Pandan Island, Snake Island, a long and narrow curvaceous sandbar, Meara, Marina, Luli Island (from lulubog-lilitaw, depending on the tide), Senorita Island, where lapu-lapu breeds, Arriceffi where Dos Palmas Resort is, and private islands and unnamed ones. We went to two, Pandan and Snake Island, and the third site was not an island but a floating platform to dive from to view the magnificent Pambato Reef. It was worth it giving up an island, but too bad that we didn't have underwater camera. Except for the sheer depth and dimension of the Australian Great Barrier Reef, where the coral columns tower like the skyscrapers of NYC and the spaces between them seem like plunging canyons, this was just as spectacular in color and diversity. Anyway, you have to see it, it's indescribable.

I think you can spend nine days in Palawan and easily not be bored, from weekend to weekend, and combine moderate accommodations in strategic locations for touring, and stay a night in the expensive resorts for spa treatments and pampering. Definitely stay in Puerto Princesa to get the vibe of the city and the island. Staying in the top resorts isolates you from the local ambience, and it's cheaper to book tours locally. The prices are standard and the operators are well regulated, and they follow the rules! They're afraid of penalties because their Mayor enforces them. This mayor, Edward Hagedorn, has been mayor since 1992, and is supposedly ineligible to run for office in the 2010 elections, having reached term limit, however one term was disqualified for counting because his election then was a recall election and does not qualify as a term. Whatever, it's all legal reasoning, and anyway he's running this year, but before his election in 1992 he was a gambling lord, running *jueteng,* and his family had been big loggers denuding the Palawan forests. As Mayor, however, he cleaned up the city literally. It has won awards as the cleanest city. He banned gambling, stopped illegal fishing, got rid of crime, relocated squatters into permanent housing, started a reforestation program, etc., but most of all was the vision behind tourism and conservation happening now.

And he's not even native. He's from Paranaque and his father is German. He runs the city like a benevolent despot, with Christian platitudes in his speeches. He's GMA's darling because he's popular and investors and banks like him. He is such a powerful personality that no one dares question whether he's corrupt like most politicians. Anyway, the masses accepts corruption as a fact of life, they look the other way so long as they benefit too. He does have style, like he started a Festival for the Forest for the reforestation efforts, and every February 14 he officiates in the Mangrove Love Festival, a mass wedding that is held free for the couples, including reception, in exchange for the couples planting mangrove trees in the swamp and maintaining them to sustain the environment balance. How about that. Too bad I'm leaving before this event and will miss out on the unique experience.

Manila

Manila has new centers of entertainment and restaurant complexes. Greenbelt just added another mall to their complex, full of designer boutiques, Prada, Chanel, Louis Vuitton, and the like. The Skyway from the airport to Makati just opened two months ago, and it's twenty minutes to my hotel, unbelievable. Spas are cropping up everywhere. My Tagaytay tour was cancelled because my travel agent couldn't fill up the minimum, but my friend quickly offered to personally accompany me on a private tour on my return from Batanes, how lovely is that? It gained me a free day in Manila to go to places not in the formal tour itinerary. To do a Manila city tour will cost up to over P2000 to include the Chinese cemetery, to hire a driver and air conditioned car from the agency for ten hours will cost P9000, the taxi will do up to six hours for $3000. I negotiated P500 with a taxi to take me to the Chinese cemetery, wait a few minutes, then to stop by Malacanang for a few minutes then drop me off in Ongpin to do Chinatown and Quiapo. It was a perfect day.

Ongpin had cleaned up its act since a few years ago when I tried to visit and the place was literally buried in garbage. Now it smells of sizzling barbecue from the sidewalk vendors, and of other creatures cooking on the fryer or grill that look so inviting it makes you hungry. It has all the colors of the rainbow with vegetable and fruit stands crowding the sidewalks and infiltrating the street, people and tricycles and jeepneys jockey with one another to get through. It's the Chinese New Year, the year of the Tiger, Gung Hay Fat Choy!, so people are milling about in the trinket stalls and shops buying lucky charms and amulets, and the traditional sticky rice cakes, *Tikoy,* are selling like hotcakes! Firecrackers and loud drums and noisemakers jolt you periodically. If they're supposed to drive away evil spirits, then I don't know how they do it, but the lion and dragon dance troupes manage to clear the streets briefly so they can go through and stop by many of the businesses to bring them good luck.

I forgot how big Chinatown is, and I'm happy to see that it is vibrant, crowded, exciting, noisy, colorful, and that you can't go wrong with the food whether purchased from the street or from a white table-clothed air conditioned restaurant. I stopped by for lunch in a seafood restaurant. You can choose your entree from almost two dozen tanks of live catch, from different fish species, to clams and other shellfish, lobster, stone crab, eel, sharks, prawns, etc. Then I segued to Quiapo and passed the Basilica of the Black Nazarene, its courtyard a marketplace selling the black nazarene and religious icons, candles, food and drinks, fortune tellers, then on the way to the souvenir shops *sa ilalim ng tulay,* you pass vendors of all persuasion, selling everything from auto parts to fake Italian jewelry. I was able to purchase an outlet adaptor for my electric converter for P85, the currency exchange is P46.29 to $1 today, bad for the dollar, good for the Peso. The TV is peppered with maudlin ads by candidates, appealing to the emotions of the masses.

I hear y'all are buried in the white stuff, heh heh

Ilokandia

This has got to be the turning point in this grand tour, opening my eyes and heart to the Ilokano people, I mean their history is the stuff of epic novels. There are so many revolutionary heroes among them (and so many infamous ones too) and the heroic stand at Tirad Pass should compare with any great stands for independence in the history of the world. And they knew what battles to fight early on in the colonial period. I take my hat off to the Basi revolt of 1807, when they defied the Spaniards after they prohibited the distillation of the regions favorite sugar cane liquor. Like, "Hey you may oppress us, but you cannot take our *basi* away." They were subdued, of course, and the ring leaders decapitated, but they made their point.

Fort Ilokandia Resort remains a Marcos monument in spite of confiscation by the government and privatization with Chinese management. The buildings are well-designed, patterned after colonial residential architecture and the grounds and beach are beautiful, but the decor is tacky and the service and food are lousy. The art works on the walls are blow ups of pictures of Imelda with various world dignitaries and of winners of various beauty contests and such. I played golf twenty minutes away in Paoay, near the Malacanang North, another Marcos monument, on the edge of Paoay lake. The view was beautiful, but just as the farmland was parched due to El Nino, the fairway had lost its turf, and on the holes along the edge of the lake you are hitting on sand fairways. The greens are kept intact but slow. I was the only one on the course and my caddy, and my game was pitiful.

I caught the end of the Pamulinawen festival and the start of the Guling Guling Festival, which was very nice and colorful. Vigan heritage block will be very lovely once reconstructed, very old world, and the few colonial houses that are restored are transformed into restaurants and boutiques and at night the block is lighted with pretty lanterns. Pagudpud which is the northermost edge of Luzon has a long stretch of white beach and several small resorts with restaurants. Sunbathing on the beach and soaking in the sea is fine but the surf in these parts is voluminous, with strong undertow, and can be dangerous.

The local cuisine is great, I tried the Ilokano *delicacies bagnet, poque-poque, tinubon,* their *empanada*, *insarabasab*, and their anise roll called *biscocho* is wonderful.

Imelda had been sighted here to attend the Guling Guling fiesta, She's running for congresswoman. I took a private tour with a guide and driver and the driver says that he used to be in the army and served in the Marcos Malacanang for ten years. He told a lot of stories about politics then, and whether or not he's lying, they're pretty fantastic.

The Banaue Rice Terraces

The rice terraces are all over the mountains. Wherever there is a water source there are rice terraces, big and small to spectacular. The most amazing are found in Batad, which are panoramic and amphitheater-like, but the access requires a two-hour hike over uneven and steep terrain. Banaue, by comparison, has a comfortable and easily accessed view point. They are over 2000 years old, chiseled into the mountain by people who crossed the land bridges from China and Taiwan and settled here. The people do have Chinese features, which makes the theory credible, but there are critics to this theory who negate the land bridge approach and who claim that the Philippines arose from the bottom of the sea, pushed out by volcanic eruptions and earthquakes from the thin Pacific crust. Whatever. The fact is that there are rice terraces here.

Preserving the terraces is a high-maintenance endeavor that requires everyone in the family, including children, to work the fields. The risers need to be weeded regularly, the soil manually tilled because carabaos cannot be brought to the high elevation, the terrace dams need constant repair and upkeep, and the water canals and irrigation system guarded vigilantly to prevent abuse of use by others sharing the community resource. Because the elevation brings only one growing season, harvesting is a delicate practice that wastes no grain. The rice stalks are cut in single stems with a special tool, not swept cut by a scythe, then each strand is tied together and stored with the husk until ready to use. Only two to three days' worth of grain is processed at a time. It's back breaking work.

Built before Spanish colonization, the rice terraces is a proud symbol of Filipino heritage, but modernity and development is threatening it.

The saddest thing is the once magnificent mountain surrounding the terraces is almost completely denuded of virgin forest and covered entirely by cogon grass. One could weep. The birds no longer sing in these mountains, and the Kamagong is endangered. The deer is gone and few wild boars roam. All the grand mountains and forests of the Philippines have been raped and looted for centuries and the abuse continues with unchecked logging, commercial development, settlement, mining, corporate plantations, irresponsible leaders and politicians, you name it. The indigenous peoples have been driven from their habitat and forced into begging, and to give up their life style, identity and traditions to work for survival in low paying jobs in the general community.

Hello!

Back to Manila and I am spending my last week immersed in its art and cultural heritage scene and am very blown away by the creativity, pride, and patriotism expressed by our artists intent on re-"righting" and retelling our history. Though this scene does not yet reach or interest the masses, who continue to swarm in shopping malls and movie houses, and watch Wow-Wow-Wee on TV, the movement is there and we can hope that some financier with a vision will underwrite a popular movie or TV show or something someday and spread the message incubating in this small and elite group. Until recently we didn't have museums or cultural centers, and grudgingly I credit the Marcos regime and Imelda for setting herself as patroness of the arts, and who laid the infrastructure for showcasing our art and culture. The Philippine National Museum is rich with the display of our patrimony. Its current exhibit is about the re-examination of Philippine-American relations during the Philippine-American War years, 1898-1915.

By the way, it's only recently that the US Library of Congress has changed the catalogue label to Philippine-American War from its previous nomenclature of Philippine Insurrection. It is a revelation, how a simple labeling change could change its definition. Both sides should be educated so we can see each other more clearly and deal with each other with mutual respect and equality. The rich here are also starting to give back and are sharing their art and artifact collections, through their museums that are open to the public. The Ayala Museum is world class, and so are the Lopez and the Yuchenco Museums. The latter has a wonderful exhibit of Santiago Bose and the historian and journalist Carlos Quirino. The Metropolitan Museum of Manila likewise has a large collection of modernists. The Cultural Center puts up superb productions. I saw Rody Vera's adaptation of Chekhov's Three Sisters, *Tatlong Mariya*, directed by Loy Arcenas. It's two and a half hours long but you forget the time, it's that good and absorbing. I'm going to see the neo-ballet on Friday. The Tourism Department is doing a great job of restoring heritage sites and creating heritage tours. I was engulfed with nationalistic fervor in the Aguinaldo Museum and wept. These heritage tours are made available to schoolchildren but I don't think it is done systemically. Unfortunately, there are very few visitors to the museums and the cultural center.

Well, I was paying for my ticket at the Yuchenco museum today and here comes Krip rushing out of the lobby. I had to act fast to call his attention and he paused, and didn't recognize me. I of course have googled his picture way back when Nancy sent a link about him that's why I recognized him. I had to refresh his memory about Larap, and then he remembered that he was sending us emails, but lost contact. He apologized that he was rushing to get somewhere, and didn't pause to ask about us. I thought that was lacking in social graces, but then I was also unprepared for this encounter and wasn't fast in thinking on my feet, so I didn't come up with any bold approach like strong-arming him and sitting him down for coffee, or just collaring him to set up a meeting if he's in such a rush. I wouldn't have recognized him either if I hadn't googled his picture, and I think he remembers more Hazel and Nancy, they're contemporaries. But even my current acquaintances would be hard pressed to recognize me. I'd just left the dentist, I had no make-up or any lipstick on, It was a bad hair day, and I was in jeans and oversized shirt. I guess he's into the inner art circles here and a published and well-reviewed author. An apparition from the past, when everything was full of promise and wonder, and sadly neither of us had the prescience to seize the moment and reconnect.

About the Author

Metty Pellicer, aka Metty Vargas, Fiameta Pellicer, Fiameta Vargas, is a grandmother, mother, woman, and a doctor. She was born in the Philippines and immigrated to the US in 1967. She was married to John Pellicer for thirty-five years until his death from coronary heart disease in 2004 at age 58. English is a second language for her, but she also speaks Tagalog and Bicolano, and is gaining proficiency in Spanish. She lives in Atlanta, Georgia with her twenty-year old cockatiel, which still asks anyone who whistles to it, "Did you fart?"

CPSIA information can be obtained at www.ICGtesting.com
Printed in the USA
LVOW07s1053160115

423129LV00003B/6/P